Plain Talk on
LUKE

Plain Talk on
LUKE

by

Manford George Gutzke

ZONDERVAN
PUBLISHING HOUSE OF THE ZONDERVAN CORPORATION
GRAND RAPIDS, MICHIGAN 49506

PLAIN TALK ON LUKE
Copyright © 1966 by
Zondervan Publishing House
Grand Rapids, Michigan

Twelfth printing   1978
ISBN 0-310-25581-3

Library of Congress Catalog Card Number 66-18949

Printed in the United States of America

CONTENTS

Plain Talk on
LUKE

Chapter 1

INTRODUCTION

The events we are about to consider, in the gospel of Luke, occurred in the world's history a long time ago, in a strange and distant land. In the gospel of John attention is focused upon a wonderful situation where glory prevails, the center of the glory being the King of kings and the Lord of lords. But in Luke there is a revelation of Jesus Christ without that atmosphere of glory. Here is a revelation of Jesus Christ in human form, as He came into this world's history more than nineteen hundred years ago; lived, died, and rose again from the grave.

As far as their social habits were concerned, the people who lived back in those days, in that distant land, lived a very different life from men today, and yet they were human beings such as in the world now. They had the problems of making a living; they faced the difficulties involved in dealing with other people; they suffered pain; they dreaded the unknown; they grieved at the loss of those they loved. These ancient people rejoiced when they were happy, and were gladdened by good fortune, and by the blessings of providence. Young people got married, homes were established, babies were born, and people died. It was life much as it is lived today. After all they were human beings, living in a land called Judea, which is now known as Palestine.

There are many countries in that general area now, but the name Palestine will cover them all. The people involved in this account were Jews. The Jew was a person who lived in the traditions of Abraham, Isaac and Jacob, the tradition of the prophet Moses, and of the judges, Gideon and Samuel, and of the kings, David and Hezekiah, and then again of the prophets, Isaiah, Jeremiah, Ezekiel, Elijah and Daniel. The people whom Luke writes about lived in the shadow of such traditions.

But what they shared was more than tradition. They cherished their way of life as being their own. They understood they belonged to God; they knew who God was: the Creator of the heaven and the earth. They understood that God had chosen them to be His own, and that He would give Himself to them, in order that they might walk in His blessing. Because He loved them, God would be gracious to them and keep them all in the way that they should go. Because He was a holy God, He insisted that His people should be holy. This does not so much mean that they must be perfect in their outward conduct as it means that they should be single-minded in their heart's attitude toward God. He gave Himself, as it were, for them. He gave Himself to them as He watched over them. He gave their armies success against their enemies, and He overruled in their practical affairs in such a way that this little nation called Israel was truly blessed of God. The only response that could be worthy would be that they should give themselves sincerely to Him.

The Israelites actually expected blessing. They believed that the time would come when Someone of the house of David would sit on the throne, and that the whole world would be under His rule. It was not always clear in their minds that God owned all people on the face of the earth, and that He actually had all the people of the world in His mind. He had promised Abraham "I will bless thee and make thee a blessing," and He had added "In thee and in thy seed shall all nations of the earth be blessed." This may not have been always clear in the minds of the Israelites, nor later in the minds of the Jews, but it was always implicit throughout Scripture.

The Jews of whom Luke wrote were human beings, it is true, and in their human way they often had a limited view as far as God was concerned. But God had revealed Himself *to* the prophets, and *through* the prophets. He had revealed Himself to these ancient people in His promises. His Word became the written Scripture amongst them, setting forth the revelation of His will for His people forever.

All of the foregoing belongs to the history of Israel at the time of Jesus and the descendants of these people were living in and around the city of Jerusalem, which was their capital. Most of the principle events recorded in the life of the Lord Jesus occurred in that general vicinity.

It can be said with further reference to Israel that they were God's "peculiar" people. The word *peculiar* does not mean strange as to conduct, or of odd characteristics. Rather, it means personal, precious, or intimate. In that sense these people belonged to God in a way in which they belonged to no one else, just as your home, the house you live in, is your peculiar house. It is "peculiar" to all other houses in your city, because it is the one you live in, and to you that makes it different from all the rest.

These people were called *peculiar* in the sense that they belonged to God as a woman's wedding ring belongs to the woman wearing it.

However God did not intend this relationship to be so exclusive that others should be left out: that was never in His mind. In the Old Testament you will find in the Book of Jonah that Jonah was sent to Nineveh to preach. The people of that city had such a soul-shattering experience that they repented, and when Nineveh repented God spared them. They were not Israelites, but they were human beings, and God is the God of all the earth. This event showed that God's will is for all men everywhere. Whosoever will may come to Him, and God will in no wise cast out anyone who comes. Often the Jews themselves simply did not understand this, but it was always plainly set forth in the Scriptures.

The Jews had a traditional hope which they found in their Scriptures and held in common throughout the nation. It was the promise of God to send the *Messiah,* which the New Testament calls *Christ.* Whether you use the Hebrew word *Messiah* or the Greek word *Christ,* the meaning is "the Anointed One," the person especially appointed to a given task, as set forth in prophecy. Daniel said God would send the Messiah, whom Daniel called the *Prince,* and He would come to establish the kingdom of God. Israel had long looked for the coming of the Messiah, because He was to bring them blessing, and deliver them from the hand of their enemies.

It would not, therefore, seem unusual that when the Israelites suffered ill fortune, defeat, or were under oppression, they would begin to think that now, surely now, was the time for the Messiah to appear. The word was out, it was written in Isaiah, as they very well knew, " . . . When the enemy shall come in like a flood, the Spirit of the Lord shall lift up a standard against him" (Isaiah 59:19). Again and again it was customary in Israel's history and experience, when it seemed as though the shades of disaster were becoming darker and darker, and gloom was settling over the nation, that their hearts became conscious of that hope – this could be the time when Messiah would come!

So it was at the time of the birth of Jesus. The particular circumstances just then were very unfavorable to Israel. The country was ruled by Rome. To use the word *Rome,* and to speak of the Roman Empire usually gives us a feeling of power and glory on the human level. It is, I hope, not too much of a shock for us to remember that the Romans were merely foreigners to the Jews, and Palestine was a country thus controlled by foreigners. This control was, to the Jews, very distressing. Israel as a nation understood that they belonged to God, and that God was with them, and that God was the Creator of the heavens and the earth. And yet, as God's people, they were now subject to an alien, foreign, arrogant power.

THE PROPHETS

Now in Israel it had happened every now and again that someone would appear with a special unction from on high, someone especially gifted and empowered to preach the Word of God to men. Such a prophet would preach to this people, recalling to their attention who they were in the plan of God. The prophets reminded them that God had not chosen them because they were many, nor because they were good, nor because they were strong. God had selected this nation because of His grace in His own good will, and giving them, the Israelites, the great privilege of belonging to Him.

The prophets stressed that since the people did thus belong to God it was their duty to obey His will. This matter of *belonging* carried responsibility with it. He is a holy God, and He makes His will known to His people. "He hath shewed thee, O man, what is good; and what doth the Lord require of thee, but to do justly, and to love mercy, and to walk humbly with thy God" (Micah 6:8). This was the message of the prophets. They said, in effect: you may be going through your religious exercises, bringing your offerings to God, sacrificing your lambs, killing your oxen, offering up your turtle doves, all of which is very good, but our holy God looks on the heart, and He demands sincerity of heart and soul. As the prophets preached thus, from time to time, there would be people who would give themselves over to God in obedient response. Throughout Israel's history these were spoken of as the *remnant.*

Now such a man was preaching at the time that the story of Luke begins. He was John the Baptist, a powerful preacher, although he was just a young man. By the time he was about thirty years of age, he had become an outstanding preacher in the entire country. Whenever he preached out in an open area, for example outside Jerusalem, it was said the whole city went out to hear him. Everyone was stirred by the preaching of this zealous man, who had been controlled by the Holy Spirit since his birth. John the Baptist lived an austere life. He drank no wine, and did not eat the highly spiced foods of the people. He ate the laboring man's food, a poor man's fare. He was dressed in the style of a countryman, but he was a mighty preacher of God's Word.

JESUS OF NAZARETH

At that same time there came into public view another man, a cousin of John's, about whom Luke writes his gospel. He preached as John the Baptist preached, but He did not live as John lived. He did not wear the same kind of clothing, nor eat the same kind of food. He acted much more like ordinary, everyday people than John did. Yet John the Baptist said about Him, "Behold the Lamb of God!" (John 1:36).

This man preached the same type of message John preached, and which would have been preached by any spiritually-minded, orthodox Jewish rabbi. There is really no great difference between the teaching of the Sermon on the Mount, and the teaching of any orthodox rabbi even today. The message clearly points out the fact that the law of Moses is not fulfilled when kept by the letter. You must obey the law from the heart.

This Jesus of Nazareth, a second cousin of John the Baptist, went about doing good, and the works He performed during the time of His short public ministry were astonishing. He worked miracles. Amazing things happened just at His word, and some of them are reported by Luke. Jesus could speak a word, and a man's disease would be gone; He could speak a word, and a man's mind would be restored, whole; He could speak a word, and a furious storm at sea would be calmed. All men were amazed to see that He could speak just a word, and a man who had been in the grave four days, arose and walked out of the tomb.

People found it hard to believe these mighty works, yet they were done openly to be seen. Great multitudes went out to hear him, and at one time He fed as many as five thousand persons with just a few loaves and a few small fish – an astonishing thing! Another time He fed four thousand.

After about three years of preaching, this young preacher was arrested as a disturber of the peace, arraigned before the Jewish Court on charges of being a blasphemer because He claimed to be the Son of God. This charge He did not deny. He was then brought into the Roman Court and accused there of being a traitor, of attempting to set up a kingdom against Caesar. Again, this charge He did not deny. Both charges were falsely presented, falsely sustained, and the decisions were unfair, and even contrary to their law in each case. But He accepted quietly the final decision and penalty. Indeed, He had warned His disciples beforehand of what was going to happen. So He was crucified, in company with two other men, condemned to die as He was.

Three days after His death, a startling rumor began to spread through the city of Jerusalem. People said He was alive. Such news was ridiculous, to be sure, yet the claim persisted throughout the city. His apostles were humble folk, but their integrity was well-known: they were sincere men whose words could not be doubted, and they publicly affirmed that Jesus was alive. Astonishing! Surprising! Disturbing!

Despite all contrary ideas the apostles reported that He was alive. They affirmed they saw Him for the space of forty days: more than a month, nearly six weeks. They said that from time to time the Lord Jesus would appear and spend some time with His disciples. He would talk with them. He even ate with them. He invited them to handle Him, and see the wounds He had sustained at Calvary. "Behold my hands and my feet, that it is I myself: handle me, and see; for a spirit hath not flesh and bones, as ye see me have" (Luke 24:39). Thus He showed Himself alive by many infallible proofs, confirming the conviction in the hearts of His disciples that He was actually raised from the dead. The reason this was such a tremendous truth was the fact that if He could be raised from the dead, others would also be raised. Thus heaven is real: God is real: the spiritual world is real!

At the end of the forty days, in full view of them all, He was taken up into heaven in a cloud. "And while they looked stedfastly toward heaven as he went up, behold, two men stood by them in white apparel; Which also said, Ye men of Galilee, why stand ye gazing up into heaven? this same Jesus, which is taken up from you into heaven, shall so come in like manner as ye have seen him go into heaven" (Acts 1:10,11). In this gospel Luke adds the further word spoken by Jesus before He ascended up into heaven: "And, behold, I send the promise of my Father upon you: but tarry ye in the city of Jerusalem, until ye be endued with power from on high" (Luke 24:49).

THE WITNESSES

After that the important thing was to wait as the Lord had commanded. The disciples went back to Jerusalem, and spent ten days there, in an upper room, waiting for the promise of the Father. These people had been with Him for three years as He went about preaching and healing. They had been with Him when He was crucified, and had now been with Him for six weeks after His Resurrection. These men were convinced that Jesus was alive. But they were not yet ready to witness. They needed the power which would come when they received the Holy Spirit.

Then came Pentecost when the Holy Spirit came into the hearts of the believers. At this time God came to abide in them in a way of which they were truly conscious, really aware. His coming in this new and special way transported them into joy, peace and comfort. Their whole lives were changed, their whole inward experience was a new one, with true peace of mind and heart. There was joy of spirit, abiding confidence, sure faith, bright hope of what God would do. And God did work in and through them, as they rejoiced in Him.

When people are thus filled with the Spirit of God something becomes obvious to others. Their neighbors and friends look at them and sense something different. "What are you so happy about?" they will ask. "You look as if you had just inherited a fortune." The answer to that would be, of course, "I have!" For every believer, filled with the Spirit of God, is rich indeed. Not rich in money, but rich in quietness of mind and heart, rich in peace that no man can take away. There is richness of joy, a lack of worry, as well as security for the future. Christians will die like other people, it is true, but they don't stay dead. When death takes a believer in the Lord Jesus Christ, that saved soul goes right into the presence of God: "Absent from the body – present with the Lord."

Just think of the testimonies these early believers could and did give! They would testify as to how wonderful it was to have God living within them. And if people scoffed and insisted that the disciples were sinners like the rest of mankind, the reply was swift, clear and positive. They could affirm, as believers do today, that they *were sinners but are now saved by grace:* Christ Jesus had died for them, and even though their sins were as scarlet, His precious blood made them as white as snow. They had their own way of praising God and thanking Him for sins forgiven.

When a scoffer would call attention to the fact that Christians had to endure adversity just as other people did, the reply again would be quick and positive. They would admit to the fact of testing and trial, of having to work and live like other people, the difference being in the peace and confidence of a calm inward rest in Christ. "God will take care of us," they would say, "and when we leave this life, we go straight into His presence."

Other persons observing the early Christians might think to themselves, if only I could have a faith and a peace like that! If any Christian were approached with such a question he could say it was a free gift from God, and it is for anyone who will put his faith and trust in Jesus Christ, crucified and risen from the dead. Jesus Christ? The name would focus the thinking of people on Jesus of Nazareth and then the way was open for the telling of the full story, just as we have been going over that glorious record in our study thus far. And this message continues to bring blessing to the hearts of men to this day.

Because Jesus rose from the dead, believers do not have to remain forever in the grave. They will be raised from the dead; they can be in the very presence of God, and more than that, God will come now and dwell within the hearts of His people. They can be as children, adopted into the family of God. He is willing to become their Father in very truth, and His Holy Spirit can be in their hearts to comfort them day by day.

People have not changed, for human nature is the same now as it was then. Men and women, who see communion with the living Lord manifested in someone, still long for the same experience. The marvelous truth is that all any person needs to do is to put his faith in Jesus Christ, trusting in Him . . . and another soul is brought to God. He will be another person who experiences the joy of sins forgiven, the peace of the indwelling Spirit and the joy of having nothing between himself and his loving Father in heaven. How wonderful to know that whether one lives a long time or a short while here on earth, heaven is always home. In this world believers are pilgrims and strangers, but one day they shall be at home. Then what joy and peace, what gladness of heart, singing and praising God around the throne!

Even before that home-going, think of the opportunities for testimony as others watch and see a new kind of life! People will say, "He is a kind person; she is a good woman. They help the poor, they have compassion on the weak; they can be trusted, for they are honest." Thus they will see the marks of righteousness, and their reaction will be to long for the same kind of life. This becomes a sort of endless chain, for the process begins all over again. A sinner believes; Christ forgives sin; the Holy Spirit comes to dwell within the redeemed and cleansed heart, and another is saved. This story goes on and on, as it did after that first day of Pentecost.

Wherever the disciples went, their shining faces attracted attention. They were always on exhibition and their quiet, confident trust in God made people "homesick for God," as it were. Thousands upon thousands came to know Him through the witness of these first Christians. The religious leaders of that day did not like this. So persecution of the believers began. The disciples were told their preaching and teaching was unsettling the community, disturbing the peace, and they must keep quiet. Repeated efforts to repress these early Christians failed. So they were threatened with beatings and other punishment, but added threats only brought forth added testimony – always with the same results.

Men and women would see how these Christians (as they began to call them) suffered, yet remained strong, self-controlled and peaceable under persecution. So one after another longed for something like this, and again souls were won for Christ. It was said that Paul belonged to that company of people who had turned the world upside down. All over Palestine, all over Mesopotamia, out over Asia Minor, down into Africa, across to Europe and finally into Rome itself spread this remarkable story: a human being could have fellowship with God! The creator of the heavens and the earth would accept any man as His own child, would treat him as a son, and would live within his heart, in the Holy Spirit. Men could have God for their very own Companion – this was indeed a new and glorious doctrine.

The idea became prevalent that this world was not the end. Whether a person lived a long or a short time, whether he were rich or poor, fortunate or unfortunate, this world was for only a little time, whereas eternity was awaiting you. In this eternal future, you would be like the Lord Jesus, enjoying the felicity of the presence of God forever and ever.

The Christians sang hymns about this new life in Christ. They kept on telling the story, and more and more thousands believed. Persecution spread from the few who made up the first group, to many of those who became Christians through the earnest testimonies they had heard. The more the story was told the more people believed, and so the more did the persecution spread. An increasing number of Christians were beaten and stoned. Some were killed. But always their witness was glorious. We see this in Stephen, the first martyr, who, while being stoned to death, affirmed with his face shining as the face of an angel that he was seeing Jesus Christ alive in heaven at the right hand of the Father.

THE GOSPEL WRITTEN (1:1-4)

As time went on, Paul probably covered the whole Mediterranean world in that first generation. It was important that this marvelous and true story should be kept accurate as it was retold again and again. The events recorded about Jesus of Nazareth, the Son of God, incarnate in human form, must be told exactly as they happened. As long as the first apostles were telling the story, they could be accurate, for they had been eyewitnesses, and the main events of the story were well-known to them. But it became a matter of concern that when the apostles were dead, who would know the true story of Jesus of Nazareth? Luke recognizes the problem very frankly in the first four verses of his gospel:

> Forasmuch as many have taken in hand to set forth in order
> a declaration of those things which are most surely be-

lieved among us, Even as they delivered them unto us, which from the beginning were eyewitnesses, and ministers of the word; It seemed good to me also, having had perfect understanding of all things from the very first, to write unto thee in order, most excellent Theophilus, That thou mightest know the certainty of those things, wherein thou hast been instructed.

It should be kept in mind that at the time of the writing of this gospel there were doubtless thousands of Christians all over the Mediterranean world, in Palestine, up in Asia Minor, across in Greece, and all the way over to Italy, as well as down in Africa. Thus over a wide area there were many people who believed this story of the good news of God's love.

It is entirely possible that Luke never saw Jesus Christ, and in all probability he was not present when many of these events took place. Luke was not a Jew, but rather a Gentile. He came into the apostolic company just when Paul went into Europe. It is at this point the Book of Acts begins to be written in the first person. Until then the writer talked of Peter, Paul and others, referring to them always as *they, them* or *he* (Acts 16:10). Expositors agree generally that this was when Luke joined the apostolic company. Luke was a physician, as we know from Colossians 4:14, where Paul speaks of him as "Luke, the beloved physician." This man was trained as a doctor and would see all that was going on, not as a priest, but as a layman unaccustomed to stereotyped religious ideas. Luke came face to face with the story of Jesus of Nazareth. He heard the claim that this Jesus Christ was virginborn, the only begotten Son of God.

The most normal thing for a doctor to do would be to inquire, to question, in order to find out all he could about the authenticity of such accounts. And that is what is implied here, as he says "those things which are most surely believed among us," referring no doubt to Peter, John and James who were indeed eyewitnesses. We do not know how many people wrote about the life and works of Jesus. We have the record of four – Matthew,

Mark, Luke and John – but there may well have been others.

Luke's word: "It seemed good to me also, having had perfect understanding of all things from the very first, to write . . ." does not mean that Luke had been with them from the very first and had such perfect understanding of the times when Jesus was born because he was there. No, it means rather that Luke had inquired, checked, informed himself, making it a point to go back to the events of those early days that he might ascertain from the testimony of reliable witnesses what had actually happened. Thus he would have a clear picture of what had taken place and could speak truthfully of his "perfect understanding." Luke promised his friend, Theophilus, that he would set things down in seriatim fashion – first, second, third, fourth – "that thou mightest know the certainty of these things" as far as was humanly possible. Luke wanted to be sure that his friend should have an accurate, comprehensive story of all that had happened. It can be helpful to remember that this was his purpose as he prepared the material for what we now call the gospel according to Luke. There need be no doubt this is a carefully checked and edited report.

Since Luke was a doctor, certain aspects of the story of Jesus of Nazareth would be even more amazing and astonishing to him than to an ordinary layman. The beginning and the ending of the life of Jesus of Nazareth especially were extraordinary. The circumstances were different from anything Luke would ever have seen or known. Certainly the first thing which would attract the attention of a physician would be the virgin birth. We shall study this in detail in our next chapter.

The question could be raised, How would Luke find out about the virgin birth? Who would tell him? The fact is there is no record of the death of Mary, the mother of Jesus. It was recorded that she was at the cross and also in the ten day prayer meeting before Pentecost. Jesus Himself, while on the cross, made arrangements with

John to care for His mother, so that from then on it is likely that she lived in the household of John. In any case it would be a normal thing for this Gentile physician to talk over this amazing matter with Mary. And surely a doctor who accepted Christ would be one in whom Mary would be ready to confide!

It is noteworthy that the most fully described record of the virgin birth is given in Luke. Matthew makes it plain that Jesus was born of a virgin mother. But Luke goes into the matter more carefully: he writes more about it, and surrounds the fact at so many points with evidence that cannot be disregarded.

Again, the most vivid description of the death of Jesus is found in Luke's gospel. The close of Jesus' earthly life was not the crucifixion but rather the Resurrection with the subsequent Ascension. All this is reported in complete detail by this doctor. No one could note better than a physician how Jesus had died on that cross. The significance of the report of how, when His side was pierced with a spear blood and water ran out would be known to a doctor. Someone else might try to start the rumor of the body of Jesus being revived, as one would revive a person in a coma or stupor, but when a doctor heard of the piercing spear, the gaping wound, and the gushing forth of blood and water – he would know this meant death.

Again, the most vivid account of the Resurrection of Jesus Christ is given by Luke, and for a physician to believe that a dead body could be infused with life again, could resume breathing, and could raise the hands in blessing – this would be almost incredible. Matthew tells about the Resurrection, and there is no uncertainty in his account. This is also true of Mark and John, but when Luke speaks of it, he quotes the actual words of Jesus, which from a practical viewpoint indicates the reality beyond question: "Behold my hands and my feet, that it is I myself; handle me, and see; for a spirit hath not flesh and bones, as ye see me have" (Luke 24:39). Here is the testimony of a physician! This was no ghost; this was the living Lord! The report goes on: "And while they yet believed not for joy, and wondered, he said unto them, Have ye here any meat? And they gave him a piece of a broiled fish, and of an honeycomb. And he took it, and did eat before them." This is the kind of evidence a doctor would seek!

Scientists are always impressed by concrete evidence. There was honeycomb on the dish, and then it was gone. There was a piece of broiled fish, but it was eaten before their eyes. The disappearance of the honey and fish would establish beyond any doubt that the body of Jesus of Nazareth was actually alive and present there. Luke records in plain factual terms the account of what was told him by credible witnesses who saw it happen. The whole story is obviously convincing, and this is what Luke meant it to be when he wrote: "To whom also he (Jesus) shewed himself alive after his passion by many infallible proofs . . . " (Acts 1:3).

The writings of Luke have been notable for their dependability as historical accounts. There is a well-known example of this in the testimony of one man, a young Scottish scholar, reared and well-educated in his native land, who was able to pursue private research to satisfy his own mind about the historicity of the Bible records. He decided to devote himself to a study of the evidence he could find. He began his research feeling sure he would discover that the New Testament was not historically accurate. He did not doubt that Jesus had lived, but he felt there were inaccuracies in the New Testament records that could be proven as untrue. In the interest of truth and accuracy, this young scholar committed himself to undertake the investigation, and then make his discoveries known as a contribution to the Church.

So this young scholar went to Palestine to make an exhaustive study from the historical standpoint of the Biblical record of the New Testament events. He expected to return to Scotland with sufficient evidence to show that the records of Matthew, Mark, Luke and John – the gospels – were not reliable. This honest, diligent scholar is now known by the honored name of Sir William Ramsey. He wrote a monumental book on the gospel of Luke. Copies of this work are not commonly available and the average person probably would not have the patience to read it through; but the conclusion he reached should be accepted as evidence in any court of appraisal. Simply put, it was this scholar's documented conclusion that Luke, the beloved physician, was the most accurate historian of ancient times.

Chapter 2

THE VIRGIN BIRTH

Luke begins his gospel with the story of the birth of John the Baptist and follows this with the story of the birth of Jesus Christ. It is interesting to note how Luke tells these stories, so that the reader may better appreciate the background situation in the mind and the consciousness of the people at that time.

The birth of John the Baptist was unusual, and the birth of Jesus of Nazareth was extraordinary. Certainly the parents of John the Baptist were fully conscious of something unusual about John; and Mary, the mother of our Lord had been told that hers would be a most unusual child.

However, we are given no particular clue as to how the other members of Mary's family felt about these things, nor does the Bible make clear how much the friends and relatives of Zacharias and Elisabeth knew about the circumstances surrounding the birth of John. Luke is the only one of the writers of the four gospels who tells this story about John the Baptist. Matthew also tells the story of the birth of Jesus, but his is a much simpler story. Luke's version is more exact and detailed, and, as we have already noted, that might be expected from a physician.

THE BIRTH OF JOHN (1:5-25)

The birth of John the Baptist had nothing miraculous about it, although it was unusual. The record in itself is simple and factual.

There was in the days of Herod, the king of Judaea, a certain priest named Zacharias, of the course of Abia: and his wife was of the daughters of Aaron, and her name was Elisabeth. And they were both righteous before God, walking in all the commandments and ordinances of the Lord blameless. And they had no child, because that Elisabeth was barren, and they both were now well stricken in years. And it came to pass, that while he executed the priest's office before God in the order of his course, According to the custom of the priest's office, his lot was to burn incense when he went into the temple of the Lord. And the whole multitude of the people were praying without at the time of incense (1:5-10).

This account does not tell the actual age of Zacharias and Elisabeth, though it does note they were old, in the sense that their age would preclude any further possibility of a child being born to them. Zacharias was engaged in his duties in the temple, going through the ritual of appearing before God to sprinkle the blood of the sacrifice upon the altar, to carry the oil for anointing, to present the peace offering and the wave offering, etc. These were the various ritualistic exercises which belonged to the work of the priest.

There were many priests in the temple service, each assigned to a particular task. Evidently they rotated in these, since we are told about Zacharias that "his lot was to burn incense . . . " He was doing this on behalf of the people who came to worship. Their sacrifices had been offered and accepted, and they were praying "without" at the time of incense. This meant they were standing outside of the Holy Place. They would wait thus until the priest came out and pronounced the benediction from God. Zacharias would go in to present their worship for them, to offer up their praise to God, and would then return and announce to them God's good will and gracious forgiveness. All of this was on the course of their formal ritual of worship.

But the events of this particular service of worship on this day did not follow the usual pattern:

> And there appeared unto him an angel of the Lord standing on the right side of the altar of incense. And when Zacharias saw him, he was troubled, and fear fell upon him. But the angel said unto him, Fear not, Zacharias: for thy prayer is heard; and thy wife Elisabeth shall bear thee a son, and thou shalt call his name John. And thou shalt have joy and gladness; and many shall rejoice at his birth. For he shall be great in the sight of the Lord, and shall drink neither wine nor strong drink; and he shall be filled with the Holy Ghost, even from his mother's womb. And many of the children of Israel shall he turn to the Lord their God. And he shall go before him in the spirit and power of Elias, to turn the hearts of the fathers to the children, and the disobedient to the wisdom of the just; to make ready a people prepared for the Lord (1:11-17).

It is not surprising that Zacharias would be startled and confused at this unusual experience.

Angels are never fully described in the Bible. There may be some description of their garments, as in the first chapter of Acts, and again, when the angels were in the open tomb of our Lord, their "shining garments" are mentioned, but this is no indication whether an angel looks like a man, or what he looks like. No angel is ever described as having wings. Many beautiful cards at the Christmas season and in other printed materials portray angels with beautiful, wide-spreading wings, but the idea is not Biblical.

Cherubim and Seraphim are mentioned in the Bible. We do not know who or what they are, nor what the word *Cherubim* actually means. In English they would be called *Cherubs*. This word is often used for children who sing in our junior choirs, but there is no indication of the meaning of this word in the Bible. It does appear that there are certain created beings in heaven, but it is difficult to make any distinction between them, since there is so little information. The Bible speaks of Gabriel, and of Michael the archangel, but no further information is given. The Greek word used for *angel* is the word translated *messenger*. It would be correct to understand that the "messenger of the Lord" was standing on the right side of the altar of incense.

It would seem quite natural to think of the angel as looking like a man, because he was standing. However, when Zacharias saw the messenger, there must have been some outward appearance which marked him as unusual, for "he was troubled and fear fell upon him . . ." This is not fear in the sense of being terrified, but rather in the sense of awe, of being tremendously impressed by this visitor.

The angel spoke at once, saying "Fear not." No mention is made of the petition Zacharias may have been making in his praying, but it seems reasonable that he and Elisabeth could have been praying for years for a son. Graciously now came the message from God, " . . . thy wife Elisabeth shall bear thee a son . . . thou shalt have joy and gladness . . . many shall rejoice at his birth . . . " The angel revealed further that this promised son was to grow into a man of unusually deep spiritual nature.

Even before birth, John was to be under the power and influence of the Holy Spirit, and was to become a great person in the sight of God. He was to abstain from all forms of worldly indulgence, to be a man of simple habits, living an austere life for the sake of God. He was to become a great religious leader and teacher, turning many people to God, going forward in the spirit and power of Elias. The word *Elias* in the Greek and the word *Elijah* in the Hebrew are one and the same, just as people might say Thomas or Tom, for the same man. Such changes in word structure occur in different languages because of certain sounds which do not fit into the speech of a given nation. The Greeks used John for Johanan, even as today the Scots use Ian for John.

Then the messenger gave a short description to indicate that John's preaching would be the kind that would lead people into godliness, and a brief description of what such godliness in the life of the nation would mean: fathers would be fair to their children, the disobedient would accept the wisdom of the just, and people would be prepared for the coming of the Lord. Even though this was a short, glowing and stimulating promise, the reaction of Zacharias was one of doubt.

> And Zacharias said unto the angel, Whereby shall I know this? for I am an old man, and my wife well stricken in years. And the angel answering said unto him, I am Gabriel, that stand in the presence of God: and am sent to speak unto thee, and to shew thee these glad tidings (1:18, 19).

Such a response is, perhaps, quite natural, for Zacharias would be looking only at the circumstances: He was an old man, his wife an aged woman. "How can I believe this?" was his cry. The answer of Gabriel is significant: "I came from God! I stand in His presence!" This was offered as a sufficient guarantee of the validity of the prediction. As a godly man, a priest for most of his life, living close to God, Zacharias should have known better than to ask God for a reasonable explanation of His declared will and purpose.

When God told David that He was going to take one of his sons and put him on the throne forever, and all the kingdoms of the earth would be under him so that the Seed of David would sit on the throne permanently—David went back into the temple. He turned his face up to God and acknowledged before God that he was nothing. "I am a little man, I don't amount to much, but Thou art God, and Thou hast said that this thing shall be true. I am utterly astonished, but if this is Thy will, so be it." Such response was certainly acceptable to God, and shows the high level on which David lived his life of faith. But when Zacharias was told that Elisabeth was to bear him a son, he could not believe it. Confronted with this apparently impossible promise Zacharias asked "Whereby shall I know this?" He had just been told what God was about to do, but he wanted some proof. For this wavering, the chastisement of God came upon Zacharias.

And, behold, thou shalt be dumb [the angelic messenger continued], and not able to speak, until the day that these things shall be performed, because thou believest not my words, which shall be fulfilled in their season. And the people waited for Zacharias, and marvelled that he tarried so long in the temple. And when he came out, he could not speak unto them: and they perceived that he had seen a vision in the temple: for he beckoned unto them, and remained speechless. And it came to pass, that, as soon as the days of his ministration were accomplished, he departed to his own house. And after those days his wife Elisabeth conceived, and hid herself five months, saying, Thus hath the Lord dealt with me in the days wherein he looked on me, to take away my reproach among men (1:20-25).

Thus did God make Zacharias realize, in a very personal way, that He was a God of power. The people outside were expecting the ministering priest to come out with the Lord's blessing, but he tarried within until they began to murmur in amazement: "they marvelled that he tarried so long." When Zacharias finally emerged, he had to make signs with his hands, for all power of speech had failed. They knew then that he must have had a vision from the Lord. As a result of what had happened between God and himself Zacharias was dumb, and this loss of speech continued until the baby was born.

THE BIRTH OF JESUS (1:26-38)

And now we come in our study of Luke to the birth of Jesus of Nazareth.

And in the sixth month the angel Gabriel was sent from God unto a city of Galilee, named Nazareth, To a virgin espoused to a man whose name was Joseph, of the house of David; and the virgin's name was Mary (verses 26,27).

"And in the sixth month" refers, of course, to the pregnancy of Elisabeth. There has been much questioning and a good deal of excitement over various English translations of the word *virgin.* The word used in the original comes from the Hebrew, meaning a *young woman* or a *young maiden.* It will be claimed that this word does not necessarily mean a virgin in the physical sense of the word, or "retaining her virginity." They say the Greek equivalent, *alma,* means, by its very form, a *young woman,* or a *young unmarried woman.*

The weakness of this argument can be felt immediately when attention is given to the culture in which this language developed. Actually, when the Hebrews talked about a young unmarried woman, they meant just exactly what we mean when we use the word *virgin.* To them a young, unmarried woman was a virgin, and a virgin was a young, unmarried woman. They had no special word for what we call, technically, a *virgin.* Hence when those who try to defame the Scriptures make a big to-do about this translation, and claim the translation should use *young woman,* no significant change would occur. Translators could use the word *maiden,* and mean the same thing. No doubt Mary was a young woman, probably in her teens. If she were older than that, she would likely have been married, since it was the custom of Jewish parents to unite their young people in marriage after they came to adolescence. Thus this young girl was engaged or espoused to Joseph, but they had never lived together as man and wife, according to the customs of the land. This is what is meant when it is written that the daughter of Jephthah mourned her virginity (Judges 11:38, 39), when her father was to have her put to death because of his foolish vow. The story in Matthew and in Luke makes it plain that Mary was a virgin in the sense in which that word is used today.

> And the angel came in unto her, and said, Hail, thou that art highly favoured, the Lord is with thee: blessed art thou among women (verse 28).

The Jewish people were expecting a Messiah. They were looking for a certain person to be born among them whom God would use to deliver them. He was called, in the Old Testament, *The Messiah,* and in the New

Testament, *Christ.* Every Israelitish woman cherished in her heart the hope, as a young girl, that she might become the mother of the Messiah. He would be the first-born son, and this old tradition lived in the hearts of the young women, who longed that their first-born son might be the God-promised deliverer.

There is a passage in the Old Testament Scriptures which says Elijah must go before Him, meaning that Elijah must return and go before the Messiah. Even today at certain seasons of the year in an orthodox Jewish home, when the family sits down to a ceremonial meal, they always leave one chair near the door empty. Often there is an extra place set at their table. These arrangements are to honor Elijah, when Elijah comes.

Throughout Jewish history this expectation of the Messiah is found. Moses had said there would arise among them a prophet greater than himself. So, when the angel came to Mary and said, "Thou art highly favoured . . . blessed art thou among women," she could well have been aware of the possibility that this would now be a fulfillment of the expectation among the women of her nation. This would be why the angel was telling her that she was especially chosen by God!

> And when she saw him, she was greatly troubled at his saying, and cast in her mind what manner of salutation this should be. And the angel said unto her, Fear not, Mary: for thou hast found favour with God. And, behold, thou shalt conceive in thy womb, and bring forth a son, and thou shalt call his name JESUS. He shall be great, and shall be called the Son of the Highest: and the Lord God shall give unto him the throne of his father David: And he shall reign over the house of Jacob for ever; and of his kingdom there shall be no end (1:29-33).

At any rate the promise to David was now to be brought to fulfillment right here. Mary was of the house of David, and because she was in that family, it was possible for her to become the mother of the Messiah.

The startling nature of this pronouncement aroused a great question in Mary's mind.

> Then said Mary unto the angel, How shall this be, seeing I know not a man? (1:34).

At first glance Mary's question seems to be like the doubt of Zacharias. Yet there must be some difference between these two cases since Zacharias was disciplined for his doubt, and Mary was not. Apparently there was a real difference in the situations of these two people before God. In the first place, Zacharias was an old man, married for years, with a long experience of service to God and blessing from God, and the promise made to him was not really as startling as was this one to a young, modest, unmarried girl. In other words, it seems that it would have been easier for Zacharias to believe than for Mary. If anyone has difficulty in believing the record of the virgin birth of Jesus of Nazareth, there may be some slight comfort in the fact that Mary questioned in those first few moments. Mary said, in effect, "this is impossible. I am not married. I know not a man."

> And the angel answered and said unto her. The Holy Ghost shall come upon thee, and the power of the Highest shall overshadow thee: therefore also that holy thing which shall be born of thee shall be called the Son of God. And, behold, thy cousin Elisabeth, she hath also conceived a son in her old age: and this is the sixth month with her, who was called barren (1:35, 36).

And then the angel added something which has been quoted far and wide always to the blessing of all God's children.

> For with God nothing shall be impossible (1:37).

Jesus came in accordance with prophecy, fulfilling to the letter what was said about Him. But when she was told how He would come as her child, Mary was bewildered and troubled, asking, "Can this be true, possibly true?" Gabriel reassured her by saying: "With God nothing shall be impossible." When God moves into a situation, and takes control, He can do anything He will, for He is Lord of all.

THE MIRACLE INVOLVED

Often the authenticity of this portion of Scripture is questioned on the ground it involves something impossible. It should always be adequate by way of answer to focus attention at this point: the questions asked by such students are similar to Mary's question. This is what she wanted to know. In her case she asked Gabriel: "How can those things be?" It is helpful to note how Gabriel told her that God was going to take care of this matter, and with Him *nothing* was impossible. Since Gabriel did not explain what was going to happen to Mary, it would seem quite out of line for any professor to undertake to explain those things!

Yet we can profit by further consideration of this important matter of the virgin birth. Let us begin by asking, What is the actual proportion of miracle involved in this incident? It will be seen that the account is not fantastic. There are fanciful stories of the deeds of gods and goddesses in mythology. Such an one is the story in Greek mythology concerning the origin of Athena, goddess of wisdom. Zeus was considered as the father of all the gods. Once Zeus had a terrific headache which lasted for three days. After much agony his head split open and out stepped Athena, fully clothed and armed. Now there is a story for you! This sort of happening is common in the myths of the gods of the Greeks.

But there is nothing like that in the gospel story of the birth of Jesus Christ. The biological facts of conception are doubtless commonly known. A cell in the body of the mother is quickened, brought to life when an infinitesimal part of the father's body, too small to be seen, except with a microscope, joins the cell of the mother's body. Mary's pregnancy apparently was normal in every respect save one: instead of the life of the father joining the life of the mother to bring life to the Child, it was the creative act of God that gave life to the body of the mother. The Scripture reveals that God created man and woman in the first place, giving them life by His power. The generations of the body of Jesus of Nazareth as an infant in the body of Mary is a similar creative work of God. The story of the virgin birth is credible to anyone who believes God gave life to Adam and Eve. What we have in these accounts of the birth of Jesus of Nazareth as set forth in Matthew and Luke is simply another new creation.

Actually, in many ways, the creation of Adam was the more wonderful, because in that case God took the dust of the earth and fashioned a body, and breathed into the nostrils of that body the breath of life. That is really a more amazing story than this one in which the power of God came upon a virgin and vitalized a cell in her own body so that it grew into a human body even as in any conception. Everything else in this birth seems to have occurred in a normal manner. Jesus of Nazareth was born as any child was born. There was nothing peculiar about it, beyond what has already been noted about the generation of life by the power of God. Jesus of Nazareth was begotten as the Second Man. The Bible speaks of Adam as the first man, and of the Second Man as the Lord from heaven. The work of creation that produced Adam, whose life is in our bodies as human beings today, is the same kind of creation involved in the generating of the body of Jesus of Nazareth. The babe of Bethlehem was different from us however in that His life was the life of God, and so was sinless; whereas in us is the life of Adam which is sinful.

All consideration of this amazing account should recognize that one cannot *convince* an unsaved, an unregenerate human being of the virgin birth. If a man does not believe in God, he has no basis upon which to substantiate any belief about the virgin birth. The premise must rest in God. There is nothing on which to ground such faith, if there is no God. Mary believed in God as the God of her nation. In her faith in Him she was able to believe He was all-powerful, and could do anything He willed. The story is just that simple in the last analysis: Mary believed and yielded herself to God for His divine purposes with confidence that He could do as He would. Unfortunately and tragically in the world today there are many people who call themselves Christians and who would be hurt if they were questioned as to their sincerity, who hold that this doctrine of the virgin birth is either untrue or unimportant. In all candor it should be noted that Luke leaves no question about the implications of the account he has written.

The Bible tells about the birth of the Lord Jesus Christ in two passages: the gospel of Matthew and the gospel of Luke. In each case the Word affirms plainly the fact that Jesus was born of a virgin. There is no question about it, no loophole which permits even the slightest doubt. Anyone reading these two accounts, whether he believes them or not, would have to agree that the plain record clearly reports Jesus Christ was born of a virgin mother.

The virgin birth was admittedly the faith of the Early Church. The Apostles' Creed affirms it in plain language:

> I believe in God, the Father Almighty, Maker of heaven and earth; and in Jesus Christ, His only Son, our Lord, Who was conceived by the Holy Ghost, born of the Virgin Mary . . .

This creed goes on to affirm His suffering under Pilate, His death, His Resurrection, etc. In that short statement, in that compendium of the doctrine of the apostles, there are two clauses about His virgin birth. The Apostles' Creed is commonly accepted as being the standard digest of the beliefs of the early Christian Church, the beliefs of the apostles. And this statement makes it clear that the Early Church held, as taught by the apostles, that Jesus Christ was conceived by the Holy Ghost and born of the Virgin Mary.

The doctrine of the virgin birth is supported by aspects of logic within itself. It makes Jesus Christ the *only-begotten* Son of God. The Scriptures speak of believers being begotten of the Word, and begotten of the Spirit, but the phrase the *only-begotten Son of God* is used exclusively of this One whose body was begotten by the power of God in the Virgin Mary.

Also the virgin birth makes the life on earth of Jesus Christ consistent with His pre-existence. When the Bible refers to Jesus Christ, it teaches that He was God, incarnate in human form. The truth is that the Son of God, the second Person of the Godhead, was in the Godhead forever. Before the creation of the world there was God, the Father; God, the Son; and God, the Holy Ghost, three Persons in the one Godhead eternally.

In John 17 Jesus prayed:

> And now, O Father, glorify thou me with thine own self with the glory which I had with thee before the world was (verse 5).

There seems to be no question but that the Son of God, who became incarnate as Jesus of Nazareth, lived with God before He came into this world. This is the meaning of the *pre-existence of Christ.*

When a man is born into this world, that is the beginning of that person. No one would think that person had lived before. But when Jesus was born, that was *not* the beginning of the Son of God. That was the beginning of His earthly body, which God created for a specific purpose. "A body hast thou prepared for me" (Hebrews 10:5). But He Himself was the Son of God, the *eternal* Son of God, and had always existed with the Father. If Jesus of Nazareth is considered as having been born just as a human being, there would be an impossible situation in the doctrine of His Person. He could not be born of human parents as men are, and yet be the Son of God eternally forever. If the phrase *Son of God* refers merely to an office, then no virgin birth was necessary; but if the phrase refers to a *person*, then He could not have been born as men are. As the Son of God He was one of the Trinity. This the Bible indicates plainly as He Himself affirmed:

> I came forth from the Father, and am come into the world: again, I leave the world, and go to the Father (John 16:28).

And so we see that the doctrine of the virgin birth is consistent with the pre-existence of the Son of God.

There is yet another line of argument. If the Lord Jesus was born of a virgin, as the Son of God, it would mean that He was not sinful, as was Adam, but sinless as His heavenly Father. David said, in Psalm 51:5, "Behold, I was shapen in iniquity; and in sin did my mother conceive me." And Paul points out that because Adam fell, all his progeny, all human beings, were fallen (Romans 5:12-18). Hebrews 4:15 states " . . . but [Jesus] was in all points tempted like as we are, yet without sin." This is to say that while Jesus had a body like ours, with bone and muscle and blood, lungs that breathed air, a digestive system that became hungry, a body which grew weary and required sleep, in all points He was like man, but without sin. It seems clear that for Jesus to be without sin, the virgin birth was necessary. Only in this way was it possible for Jesus to be human, and yet sinless.

John in his gospel (John 1:13) seems to describe such

a birth when he speaks of those who were " . . . born, not of blood, nor of the will of the flesh, nor of the will of man, but of God." All this could be said of Jesus of Nazareth. According to Luke's account, He was not born of blood, that is, of the mutual blood line of Joseph and Mary; nor of the will of man, that is, not conceived by Joseph because he wanted a son; but of God, for the Word tells us in Galatians 4:4, that " . . . when the fulness of the time was come, God sent forth his Son, made of a woman . . . " Jesus Christ was not born of human, physical progeneration, but by the will of God. The Scriptures are clear beyond doubt on this point.

There are still further considerations that enforce the importance of this doctrine. The virgin birth of Jesus of Nazareth implies the deity of Jesus Christ. It need not be claimed as proof, but it clearly implies this to be true. If men are to put their trust in Jesus Christ as God of very God, the virgin birth is important because it implies that He is God.

Another important consideration is that the virgin birth demonstrates the sovereign, creative work of God. This is the way in which God would work. When God in heaven wanted to produce a body for His Son, He seems to have willed it to be by His Word. This is how the world was created, and this is the way a man is saved. When Almighty God speaks His Word to the heart, " . . . that whosoever believeth in him should not perish, but have everlasting life," faith is generated that leads the soul to God.

This is called the *new birth, regeneration.* A person doesn't *feel* it, since there are no physical aspects, but there are results. From that moment on the person is different: he thinks differently, and wants to do differently. Something new really does take place, and this is the will of God for men and women. In other words, becoming a Christian is not the result of a series of natural processes that produce this kind of reaction. Becoming a Christian is hearing the Word of God and allowing the

Holy Spirit to quicken the heart, permitting the power of God to take control in the whole of life. Then when God works in a man "both to will and to do of his good pleasure" (Philippians 2:13), the man finds himself able to believe. "If any man will do his will, he shall know of the doctrine . . . . . " (John 7:17). He will have in his heart a readiness to believe. So when he has heard the Word of God, then " . . . faith cometh by hearing, and hearing by the word of God" (Romans 10:17). The Word of God is thus spoken to the soul, and God Himself brings that person to life eternal.

Something like that seemed to happen in the birth of the Lord Jesus in His human body. This did not happen to Mary without her knowledge. The angel came and told Mary, apparently working to enable her to believe. When He told Mary that she was to have a Son before she was married, she had the natural question of a carefully reared young girl, to whom this seemed impossible. When the reply of the angel was, "With God nothing is impossible," he put the name of God, the idea of God's power into her heart.

Thus it followed that when she finally grasped this marvelous thing which was to come to her, she could humbly say: "Behold the handmaid of the Lord; be it unto me according to thy word . . . " (Luke 1:38). Simply, with real faith, Mary accepted what God had commanded and promised. This is the attitude which will occur in the heart of any willing hearer.

Even if you should feel that actually you know very little, if you have heard the Word of God speaking to you, and are willing to commit yourself to God, saying *"Behold thy servant, let it be unto me according to thy word,"* this miracle of being able to believe will happen.

The heart must be willing, but when it is, God can and will save any soul who is ready to yield himself into God's hands. All that is necessary is willingness on the part of the man or woman, and God will work to save him.

Chapter 3

THE YOUTH AND BAPTISM
OF JESUS CHRIST

While being enrolled in the tax registration ordered by the Roman Government, Joseph and Mary were among their kinfolk in the little town of Bethlehem. No matter where a Jew lived, in any part of Palestine, he had to return to the place of his home, and be enrolled with the other members of his family. The whole country was divided according to the tribes, and Bethlehem belonged to the tribe of Judah. Joseph was of the house of Judah and the lineage of David, and so he needed to be in Bethlehem at this moment of Jewish history. This was outwardly a matter of routine, but nonetheless it was in the providence of God.

THE TIME AND PLACE OF BIRTH (2:1-7)

There is a prophecy in the Old Testament that says the Messiah would come from Bethlehem:

> But thou, Bethlehem Ephratah, though thou be little among the thousands of Judah, yet out of thee shall he come forth unto me that is to be ruler in Israel; whose goings forth have been from of old, from everlasting (Micah 5:2).

The actual course of events seems to have occurred in the way of providence. There are a few ideas commonly associated in the public mind with the birth of Jesus which have no real historical base. For example: no one knows when Jesus was born. It will not be a shock to thinking Christians to hear that Jesus was possibly not born on December 25. The selection of this particular date was done by the Church, at a time when the Church had a way of taking over the pagan holidays and making out of them Christian occasions.

This is what happened in the case of Easter, which was a Roman holiday belonging to the Roman culture. The Book of Acts records that when Herod put Peter into prison, he intended "after Easter to put him to death" (Acts 12:4). This was not the Christian Easter celebration, but a pagan Roman festival.

The Jewish people also have certain feasts or holidays at this time of year, the Passover Feast being one of them. Because of this it is possible to date the death of the Lord Jesus because it took place on the eve of the Passover. This feast had a fixed date according to the spring solstice, with reference to the movements of the sun, moon and things of nature. Thus when in Christian terminology Easter is mentioned, the Church thinks of the Resurrection of Jesus Christ. Easter was not originally a Christian idea, but the name of the holiday and the date in the calendar were taken over by the Church.

Much the same is true of December 25. The Assyrians had a date for the birthday of their sun god, and that date was December 25, which again was related to the movement of sun, moon and stars. Because the shortest day in the year came about this time, December 22-24, December 25 was the first day noticeably longer, and thus apparently it was chosen as the date of the birthday of their sun god. There seems to be no evidence to confirm that Jesus of Nazareth was born then, although this does not really matter to Christians. It is enough to know He came "in the fulness of time."

The place of His birth, however, is known as Bethlehem Ephratah, "the least of the cities of Judah." Luke gives a careful record of some of the happenings before and after the birth of our Lord. One of the famous aspects of this event was the fact that Jesus was born in a stable and laid in a manger "because there was no room for them in the inn." This does not mean quite the same as if a baby were born in a stable today. Generally speaking, most of our modern stables would be very undesirable as a living place for a family with a newborn infant. To use a stable today as a domicile for family living would be practically unthinkable. And yet even now in some countries of Europe, for example, in many rural areas the house and the stable are sections in one building, with the house at one end and the stable at the other. I can remember as a boy in Manitoba, Canada, seeing how some of the European immigrants built their homes. I was always intrigued, fascinated and perhaps a bit horrified to see a farmhouse built as one long building, of which one end was the house and the other end was the barn. To me this seemed terrible, and yet the people seemed to get along all right. Folks lived there and grew up in large families, in what seemed a very normal way.

At the same time there seems no doubt that when Joseph and Mary found lodging in the stable this was a sign of something less than desirable. It was a makeshift arrangement, even though it may not have been as bad as it sounds to us. It is not recorded that there was any antagonism shown toward this young couple who seem to have been the chance victims of an overcrowding due to the tax registration. And yet there seems to be an important spiritual lesson in this incident.

Did Any Know? (2:8-38)

It is salutary to note how His coming was unknown to many classes of people. But did anyone know, when this child was born, who He was? Consider several who were later to be much involved, beginning with the high priest. Jesus was only a baby at the moment, but He was to change the outlook of religious faith in the whole world. Everything the Jewish people believed and looked for was claimed to be fulfilled in this person. Certainly historians would agree that no one ever lived on this earth who made as much difference as Jesus Christ. But did the high priest know that this child who was born King, was in fact the very Christ for whom he and his nation had been looking for countless years? The answer is simply, *No!*

Did the Roman governor know that this child, who was born and laid in a manger, would be a man whose name would be the watershed of all history? His name stands at the very center of all history or all values of all time. We reckon all time up to Christ B.C., and all time since His birth A.D. His coming was as important as that! But did the Roman government know? The obvious answer again is *No.*

Why could this be so? Because God did not tell them; His revelation was not for them. He did not send the news of His coming to the religious or political leaders of the day, to the important people. If there had been newspapers, they would not have known. If there had been universities as we know them today, the professors would not have been told. If there were great units of society – military, commercial, social, political – any kind of responsible public group – not one of them would have known. This is enough to give one a sober sense of deep concern. God could do such a tremendous thing as to send His Son to die for sinners, and prominent, capable people would not even be aware of it.

It is not even as though no one knew, because some did know. Mary knew because the angel had told her. Exactly how much Joseph knew is not reported, but God had dealt with him in such a way as to make Joseph loyal to Jesus and Mary. He was an honorable man, and he had been told what God wanted him to do about taking Mary as his wife.

> But while he [Joseph] thought on these things, behold, the angel of the Lord appeared unto him in a dream, saying, Joseph, thou son of David, fear not to take unto thee Mary thy wife: for that which is conceived in her is of the Holy Ghost. And she shall bring forth a son, and thou

shalt call his name JESUS: for he shall save his people from their sins (Matthew 1:20,21).

It is true that Mary had a revelation from God, but here is the record that Joseph also heard the voice of the angel.

There were yet others who knew. The shepherds were out on the hills, guarding, caring for their flocks when an angel came to them, too. The shepherds were impressed by the angel's coming, and by the message from God which he brought about the birth of the Child sent from God, born in Bethlehem, born to be the Saviour of the whole world.

And the angel said unto them, Fear not: for, behold, I bring you good tidings of great joy, which shall be to all people. For unto you is born this day in the city of David a Saviour, which is Christ the Lord. And this shall be a sign unto you; Ye shall find the babe wrapped in swaddling clothes, lying in a manger (Luke 2:10-12).

Even as the angel spoke, a multitude of the heavenly host appeared, who gave glory to God. It may be worthwhile to note that Luke speaks of the heavenly host as *saying,* "Glory to God in the highest, and on earth peace, good will toward men" (Luke 2:13,14). This does not say they were *singing.* In fact there does not seem to be any report in the Bible of angels "singing." To be sure there is singing in heaven, but it is the redeemed souls in heaven who will sing round the throne of God. There is something very suggestive in the fact that it is the redeemed who sing, not angels (compare Revelation 5:9 "sang" with Revelation 5:12 "saying"). Surely the redeemed have the right and the incentive to sing the praise of Him who redeemed them by His precious blood, and they can say with David, "And he hath put a new song in my mouth, even praise unto our God . . . " (Psalm 40:3). "Sing unto the Lord a new song," says Isaiah (42:10), and the redeemed have a new song and a great song, of praise and thanksgiving for the redemption which is now theirs.

The message of the heavenly host has been pointed out by some to be better translated "Peace on earth toward men of good will."

The shepherds were "sore afraid," but that glorious message seemed to strengthen them, for they said:

> Let us now go even unto Bethlehem, and see this thing which is come to pass, which the Lord hath made known unto us. And they came with haste, and found Mary, and Joseph, and the babe lying in a manger. And when they had seen it, they made known abroad the saying which was told them concerning this child (2:15-17).

What an amazing fact that these simple shepherds knew! The religious leaders of the community did not know; the Roman rulers did not know; no one of prominence knew. Yet this company of shepherds, humble-minded folk, were chosen of God to be given His first message about His Son, who had come to give His life for the salvation of men. Here is a lesson for all men even as it is a comfort to the poor and the humble. No man can be proud or think highly of himself, if he would hear a message from God. Let a man be humble and honest, making no show of pomp or vanity, soberly doing his work, even as he listens in his soul for the voice of God. It is obviously not necessary to be one of the so-called *great ones* of the earth to have dealings with God. It would seem that God loves to deal with humble folk, even as Paul later made plain (I Corinthians 1:26-29).

There were yet others to whom God revealed the identity of this child. Eight days after the child had been born, Mary and Joseph were taking Him into the temple for the rite of circumcision. As they came into the temple, they were met by Simeon, a just and devout "man who was patiently waiting for the consolation of Israel." By the Holy Spirit God showed Simeon the significance of this child, and he recognized Him as the Lord's Christ. Simeon took the babe in his arms, saying, as he blessed God,

Lord, now lettest thou thy servant depart in peace, according to thy word: For mine eyes have seen thy salvation, Which thou hast prepared before the face of all people; A light to lighten the Gentiles, and the glory of thy people Israel (2:29-32).

The Scripture says that God had given Simeon the assurance that he would not die until he had seen the Lord's Christ. Now as Joseph and Mary brought this eight-day old child, Simeon knew at once that God had kept His word, and this was the Redeemer whom God had prepared to bring salvation. In gratitude he praised God as if to say "It is all right now, Lord, you can take me home."

Simeon was not the only one to whom God revealed the truth concerning Jesus of Nazareth on that memorable day. There was also in the temple a widow, eighty-eight years old, who had lost her husband seven years after their marriage. For approximately sixty years Anna had been a widow, and during that time she had served God in the temple, devoting all the time of her widowhood to the Lord's service. She was a humble, faithful believer in God, a patient, quiet, sincere, steadfast woman. When her eyes lit on this child, she took Him in her arms and gave thanks to God, "and spake of him to all them that looked for redemption in Jerusalem" (Luke 2:38).

God had revealed the significance of this great event to still other persons also. In the gospel of Matthew, it is written that certain "wise men" from the East came to inquire where was the One who had been born King of the Jews. Just who these "wise men" were is not clearly stated. That is the actual word used in the original language, but this gives no clue as to the real meaning of the term. It is the word from which *magician* comes, but it would not mean what that term means now. It is quite probable that today historians would call these men *scholars, philosophers* or *scientists*. They were probably the educated people of their day. They came from the East where learning was far advanced and where men had profound insights into many matters. This is where great philosophers are known to have lived and taught.

For the sake of accuracy it may be noted that no one knows how many Wise Men there were. Some time ago Henry Van Dyke wrote a beautiful little story of fiction about *The Three Wise Men.* This may well account for the popular impression that there were three. Some have thought a good reason for thinking there were three is the fact that three gifts are named; gold, frankincense and myrrh. It does seem apparent these were costly gifts, and thus the Wise Men were probably wealthy, perhaps even prominent men in their own country. But what that land was, or where, is not known.

In a similar way no one has ever been able to understand adequately the significance of that star in the heavens, which these men followed all the way from Mesopotamia to Jerusalem. This was a journey requiring weeks of travel, and it is difficult to understand how one star could guide them for such a length of time, and over such a long distance. The account is extraordinary and leaves much unknown to the modern reader, and yet the main point is clear: the Wise Men were led by a star. This star came to a stop at the place where the young child lay, so they were led to the right place. Obviously God was in the whole event and that is what the record is meant to show.

Despite the uncertainty as to details this account conveys much significant truth. These Wise Men evidently knew the King had been born. Herod did not know. They came to King Herod, naturally supposing that as king he would know of such an important event. "Where is he that is born King of the Jews?" (Matthew 2:2). It is true Herod was king, but he was not *born* king. He held that office having been assigned to it by the Romans as a matter of political expediency. "We have seen his star in the east," continued the Wise Men, "and are come to worship him." Without revealing his ignorance to them, Herod realized the potential threat to his own govern-

ment, and was now "troubled in spirit." He hurriedly
called in his own advisors to find out what they could
tell him concerning the prophecies about any coming
king.

> . . . he demanded of them where Christ should be born.
> And they said unto him, In Bethlehem of Judaea . . .
> (Matthew 2:4, 5).

The Bible tells the sordid story of Herod's treachery,
as he sent the Wise Men to Bethlehem, ordering them to
return, that he might know where to find the place since
he wanted to "come and worship him also."

It is common to think the Wise Men came on the same
night as the shepherds, joining others there as they wor-
shiped around the manger. This seems not to be the case.
The shepherds came on the night Jesus was born, but
the Wise Men apparently came some time later. Just how
much later is not stated, but Matthew 2:11 says "when
they were come into the house, they saw the young child
and Mary his mother, and fell down, and worshipped him:
and when they had opened their treasures, they presented
unto him gifts: gold, and frankincense, and myrrh." Apparently this was not the stable. Also the record is that
Herod, in his rage when the Wise Men failed to return,
". . . sent forth, and slew all the children that were in
Bethlehem, and in all the coasts thereof, from two years
old and under, according to the time which he had diligently inquired of the wise men" (Matthew 2:16).

Thus it would appear that whereas the coming of
the Son of God as the Babe of Bethlehem was unknown
to the leaders of society, to the prominent persons in the
community, His coming was nevertheless known to some.
Mary and Joseph, perhaps Elisabeth also, knew before
He was born. The shepherds knew. Simeon and Anna
knew. The Wise Men knew. What was publicly unknown,
and thus completely ignored, was at the same time known
as a wonderful truth by some humble and sincere individuals to whom the whole matter had been revealed.

This has a profound lesson for any generation. Popular opinion may be totally unaware of the truth of God, whereas at any time a humble spirit may be shown the reality of that which pertains to Christ.

The very night the Wise Men came to worship the young child, an angel of the Lord told Joseph that the life of Jesus was in danger, and he was instructed to "take the young child and his mother, and flee into Egypt, and be thou there until I bring thee word: for Herod will seek the young child to destroy him. When he arose, he took the young child and his mother by night, and departed into Egypt" (Matthew 2:13, 14). Without any other comment to guide the reader, it would seem this would be some time after the child had been born.

JESUS AT TWELVE (2:39-52)

The Bible certainly does not give any complete account of the childhood of Jesus of Nazareth. After the return from Egypt to Nazareth the next event on record occurred when He was a lad of twelve. No one has any specific idea of what He did during those first twelve years of His life. In accordance with the provisions of the law, in keeping with the customs of the Jewish people, at the age of twelve Joseph and Mary brought Jesus to enroll Him as a man in the community of the Jews as a national group. They put His name on the register, so to speak, as a young boy growing into manhood.

This seems to have been similar to the practice in some churches, where children are dedicated to God as infants and then they have confirmation procedures at the age of adolescence. The ceremony of confirmation means that the child was given to God in dedication, to be brought up in the nurture and admonition of the Lord, and later, when the child reaches a certain age of understanding there will be a procedure to enroll the child as a responsible believer. Thus at the time when the child can understand the doctrines concerning Christ,

His death and Resurrection, and concerning the significance of open profession of faith, he is taught in a communicant's class, with instruction also as to the duties of church membership. Upon being examined as to his understanding and his commitment to Christ, he is received into the membership of the church.

Something along this general line seems to have been involved in the ceremony of the Jews. Jesus was brought at the right age to be examined by the learned "doctors" in the temple. He would have been taught in the law, the Ten Commandments and the matters of Jewish procedure that a boy of his age should know. Just as our elders or other duly appointed church officials would examine a child today, so very likely did the elders in the temple examine Jesus. "And all that heard him were astonished at his understanding and answers" (Luke 2:47).

After they had finished with their services in the temple, Joseph and Mary started on their way home. With no modern means of transportation, no planes, no trains, no cars, only travel on foot, with beasts of burden, donkeys, to carry their necessary equipment, it would be pretty slow travel. A whole company of people would travel in a sort of caravan, camping together at night, when this was necessary. They had been on the way a day or more when Mary noticed that Jesus was not in the company. They had supposed, since this was a village and family group, that He was with some of His cousins, or other kinfolk, but a search revealed that He was not there. Finally they realized that Jesus must have remained in Jerusalem, so Joseph and Mary turned back to that city.

> And it came to pass, that after three days they found him in the temple, sitting in the midst of the doctors, both hearing them, and asking them questions. And all that heard him were astonished at his understanding and answers (Luke 2:46, 47).

When His mother found Him, she complained to Him about His conduct, in staying behind in Jerusalem while the rest of the company started on their way home. The answer of Jesus suggests that He knew the purpose of His coming into the world.

> And he said unto them, How is it that ye sought me? wist ye not that I must be about my Father's business? And they understood not the saying which he spake unto them (2:49, 50).

After this quiet and respectful answer, Jesus went down to Nazareth with them and "was subject unto them: but his mother kept all these sayings in her heart. And Jesus increased in wisdom and stature, and in favour with God and man" (2:51, 52).

Thus it is recorded that Jesus honored Mary and Joseph, being "subject unto them." This would mean He obeyed them in the usual affairs of family and home. When it is written that He "increased in wisdom and stature," it would mean He grew as a normal boy developing as a man with a character that was marked by reverence and obedience to God and respect, consideration and charity toward other persons.

PROCLAIMED THE SON (3:1-22)

The Bible reports nothing more in the life of Jesus of Nazareth for the next eighteen years. What was Jesus like at eighteen? at twenty? There is not a word. What did He do? How did He act? Not a word.

It is possible that the testimony of John the Baptist, as well as the voice from heaven on the occasion when Jesus came to be baptized, may well be taken as a tribute to the manner of life Jesus of Nazareth maintained throughout His earthly career. Matthew reports that John did not think his second cousin Jesus of Nazareth needed repentance (Matthew 3:13-17).

It is altogether likely that John the Baptist and Jesus of Nazareth knew each other closely as boys and as growing young men. Their births were just six months apart.

Their mothers as cousins were very close friends. John was to be "filled with the Holy Ghost, even from his mother's womb" (Luke 1:15). Certainly then John must have grown up conscious of the presence of God and very sensitive to spiritual matters. He could be expected to have a keen appreciation for the nature of the conduct of others. For this zealous godly preacher to feel that Jesus of Nazareth needed no repentance is evidence that His life must have been above reproach.

As John preached, people came to be baptized by him. This was a religious practice John did not invent, nor was he the only preacher who baptized. Baptism was a common religious practice in those days. It probably did not carry the same significance attached to it today, since the Redeemer had not yet shed His blood to redeem souls from sin. Its significance was probably similar to the practice of a modern day evangelist asking people to stand, or to come forward, at the end of a message. People who respond to the message are asked to come to the front of the sanctuary, and shake the preacher's hand. In those days opportunity was given, after a man had been taught of the law of God by the preacher and called to repent as John preached and felt in his heart that he wanted to obey the Word, to come to the speaker and be baptized by him. And so the preacher would baptize him as a public profession of his response to the call of God. All the disciples later, it is written, practiced this rite of baptism, though Jesus Himself did not baptize. John was such a powerful preacher affecting so many hearers that he was known as "the Baptist," or better translated "the Baptizer," in recognition of the many who came to him to be baptized in response to his preaching.

So, on one occasion when John was at the river Jordan preaching and baptizing, Jesus of Nazareth presented Himself for baptism. John shrank back from this, as it is written: "But John forbad him, saying, I have need to be baptized of thee, and comest thou to me?" (Matthew 3:14). At that time John did not know that Jesus was the

Christ. People came to ask John if he, himself, were the Christ. He said, "No, I am not: but He is coming. I am just a voice crying in the wilderness; I am just preparing the way before Him. But there is One coming after me whose shoe laces I am not worthy to unloose."

In the first chapter of John's gospel, it is recorded that John the Baptist was told by the One who sent him, namely, God, that the One upon whom the Holy Spirit would come as He was being baptized, that was the Christ, the Messiah. So when the Lord came to John for baptism, it was not because John recognized Him for who He was, but rather because he knew the kind of life Jesus of Nazareth had lived in all His thirty years. Because of this John did not want to baptize Him.

The message of John can be simply stated: *Repent!* Admit your personal need of God. Admit from your own heart that you are not worthy. Repent, and do the works meet for repentance. Acknowledge your own shortcomings before God. Anyone who would respond to the preaching and so admit his need, calling on God, John would willingly baptize. But when Jesus of Nazareth came, John knew the perfect life of this cousin of his, and was led to protest: "You do not need this: you have no need of repenting." Then he added, "I have need to be baptized of thee, and comest thou to me?" (Matthew 3:14). It would seem that in John's judgment the life of Jesus had been above reproach. But the Lord said, "Suffer it to be so now: for thus it becometh us to fulfil all righteousness. Then he suffered him" (Matthew 3:15). Perhaps the significance of this would be that it was appropriate that Jesus should publicly indicate in this way His approval of John's message; that by openly coming forward in this fashion and yielding Himself to baptism, He would be making His approval known to all.

After Jesus was baptized, the Holy Spirit came down from heaven in bodily form, as a dove. The Word does not say *a dove*, but *as a dove*. It may be quite proper to use the symbol of a dove, but one should not insist that a bird fluttered down and sat on the shoulder of Jesus of Nazareth. What the Word actually says is that the Holy Spirit came down in some bodily form which John could recognize, and he knew it was the Spirit of God. Whether it was the appearance of the form or the manner of its coming may not be clear to the modern reader, but it was in a way that enabled John to recognize Him for who He was.

> And John bare record, saying, I saw the Spirit descending from heaven like a dove, and it abode upon him. And I knew him not: but he that sent me to baptize with water, the same said unto me, Upon whom thou shalt see the Spirit descending, and remaining on him, the same is he which baptizeth with the Holy Ghost. And I saw, and bare record that this is the Son of God (John 1:32-34).

As the story goes along in John's gospel, the day after the baptism John was seeing Jesus as He walked by, and said, "Behold the Lamb of God!"

There is no reason to think that John the Baptist had called Jesus of Nazareth the "Lamb of God" before he recognized Him as Christ at His baptism. Apparently John understood that part of the work of Christ would be to die for the sins of men.

Chapter 4

TEMPTATION AND EARLY MINISTRY

Immediately after His baptism at the Jordan River by John the Baptist, Jesus of Nazareth was led into the wilderness where He was tempted by Satan. There is much to be learned in spiritual understanding by a close look at the record of this amazing experience. The temptation of Jesus followed the usual course of all temptation in this world.

COURSE OF THE TEMPTATION (4:1-13)

John in his first epistle describes the course of temptation thus:

> For all that is in the world, the lust of the flesh, and the lust of the eyes, and the pride of life . . . (I John 2:16).

Here are pointed out three ways of temptation, spoken of as the ways of "the world." The word *lust* in the New Testament does not imply anything particularly evil or crude. In common usage today that word is almost always associated with improper and immoral, oftentimes vulgar, desires. But as translated here from the Greek, it means a *very strong desire* in any area of interest. Paul uses it in Galatians 5:17, when he says, "For the flesh lusteth against the Spirit, and the Spirit against the flesh; and these are contrary the one to the other." Here the word *lust* is used of the Holy Spirit Himself.

As John describes that which is worldly, he refers to it as arising out of the very strong desires of human nature. The word "appetite" could well be used here. Although appetite is not exactly the same as lust, the strong desires of the flesh can grow into appetite. Hunger, for example, is one thing; appetite is another. It can be stronger than, and goes far beyond hunger. A man can cultivate an appetite just as he can cultivate a taste for anything, until his appetite begins to rule him. Hunger can be bad, but unsatisfied appetite can be worse.

Appetite in a general sense can rule many aspects of life. Normal interests can be cultivated out of all proportion and become dangerous when they are overweaning, highly exaggerated. The danger lies in the fact that gratification of the desires of the flesh feels good. Human existence depends upon the natural environment. The body needs food and feels hunger that causes it to seek to be filled. The body needs liquid and feels thirst which causes it to drink. There are other natural needs. There is need for respite from activity, and so one must find rest and sleep.

Now it is characteristic of sin that these normal needs or desires are developed to become overwhelming. What could have been a healthy hunger can become an appetite for that which is harmful. What could be a natural thirst can become an appetite for that which becomes a vicious habit, a craving for things which will hurt body and mind. Normal, healthful relaxation or recreation can actually become an addiction to a type of amusement or self-indulgence which can be positively evil and sinful. The whole range of natural needs and interests can be so developed into appetites that man is always being tempted to indulge himself with that which appeals to his taste and his desire, at the expense of missing the better things.

THE FIRST TEMPTATION

Luke's account of the temptation offered to Jesus of Nazareth shows that Satan first tempted Him concerning hunger, as He had been fasting for forty days and nights so that His human body would naturally want food.

> Being forty days tempted of the devil. And in those days he did eat nothing: and when they were ended, he afterward hungered. And the devil said unto him, If thou be the Son of God, command this stone that it be made bread (4:2, 3).

Something of the cunning of Satan is to be seen in that he tempted Jesus to provide food for Himself knowing that He was hungry after the long fast, whereas actually the real issue would be one of self-will. If he could get Jesus to act in His own interest he would have destroyed the witness of the Son of God. But Jesus knew how to reply:

> And Jesus answered him, saying, It is written, That man shall not live by bread alone, but by every word of God (4:4).

The truth is man does live by bread; that is, his body lives by bread, but it is also true his soul and spirit live by the Word of God, by every word that proceedeth out of the mouth of God. An obedient righteous man lives by faith, not by sight and sense. Jesus is saying here there is more to a man than his body, and He lays down a basic principle which is profoundly significant: man cannot live by bread alone. He can satisfy his physical hunger by bread, but he also lives by the Word of God in the matter of his soul and spirit. The soul must come first: spiritual interests must ever take precedence over physical interests (Mark 8:36, 37).

THE SECOND TEMPTATION

After this Satan tried another form of temptation in an appeal to the imagination. Man has ability to think, to construct, to project, and it is natural for the things of the imagination to become very appealing. Satan led Jesus to the top of a high mountain and told Him he would give Him control over all His eye could see, if He

would kneel down and worship Satan. Jesus answered
that temptation by saying,

> . . . Get thee behind me, Satan: for it is written, Thou
> shalt worship the Lord thy God, and him only shalt thou
> serve (4:8).

The significance of this temptation can be felt when
it is remembered that Christ is to become King of kings,
with all the kingdoms of the earth subject to Him. In
God's plan Christ must first suffer unto death and then
He would be raised to rule over all. Satan here is offering an easier way to reach that goal, without personal
suffering. This temptation Jesus rejected as being out of
the will of God.

THE THIRD TEMPTATION

After this Satan tried once more. He took Jesus to
Jerusalem, and Luke records:

> . . . and set him on a pinnacle of the temple, and said
> unto him, If thou be the Son of God, cast thyself down
> from hence; For it is written, He shall give his angels
> charge over thee, to keep thee: And in their hands they
> shall bear thee up, lest at any time thou dash thy foot
> against a stone. And Jesus answering said unto him, It
> is said, Thou shalt not tempt the Lord thy God (4:9-12)

In this temptation Satan seems to be appealing to the
natural pride of Jesus in proposing that He put God's
Word to the test in a way that would be very impressive
to onlookers. It is a grave warning to all to see that Satan
will not hesitate to use Scripture itself to tempt a soul
to be proud. Jesus showed that the safe procedure is to
compare Scripture with Scripture, and in all a person
does, it should always bring honor to God. Thus by following the guidance of Scripture, the Lord Jesus resisted
all temptation which had come to Him through legitimate
channels of human interest and desires.

There is yet more truth to be seen here. It should be noted that temptation itself is not sin. Many sincere and earnest Christians, who may be depressed because they are tempted, need to remember this. Such souls may be spiritually chagrined by their consciousness of temptation. Sensitive souls are inclined to feel that being tempted is evidence that their Christian life is not what it should be. It is true enough that the form in which temptation comes is sometimes an indication of weakness or of natural disposition. Satan is cunning and will suggest only that which he knows you like to do. Thus the form of temptation will vary from person to person: what would tempt one might never be a temptation to another. When it is written that Jesus was "in all points tempted like as we are, yet without sin" (Hebrews 4:15), it does not mean that Jesus Christ ever faced the temptation of intoxication. It is incredible that Jesus would ever be tempted to steal. Yet the Scripture does mean that He faced actual temptation along lines which were His needs or interests. Jesus of Nazareth probably never had in His mind evil thoughts which may come to any man who has evil within the heart. Satan would be far too cunning to tempt Jesus of Nazareth to do an unclean thing.

The temptation of Jesus thus shows that Satan is subtle, and will tempt good men through the clean things of this life. Temptation may come through considerations that are legitimate, through things that in themselves may be quite all right. It is when the whole situation is considered that it becomes clear that God is not in the action, and will not be glorified in the deed through which the temptation may come.

This truth can be seen later in His life when Jesus was tempted through Peter. As He told His disciples that He was now going to Jerusalem to be killed, Peter said:

> Be it far from thee, Lord: this shall not be unto thee. But he turned, and said unto Peter, Get thee behind me, Satan: thou art an offence unto me: for thou savorest not the things that be of God, but those that be of men (Matthew 16:22,23).

Thus Peter was proposing that Jesus avoid the very purpose for which He came into the world, that He should die to redeem sinners. And so Peter was, perhaps unwittingly, the channel for Satan's temptation. Peter presented a natural appeal to the interest of self-preservation. As stated, the temptation did not involve an unclean act or any deceitful purpose. Yet it was a very real temptation that actually threatened the whole salvation work of God.

Temptation in itself may not involve overt sin. It is yielding to temptation that is sin. It is coveting the thing through which temptation comes that is the dark sin which stains the soul. It is the longing for the suggested act or motive or plan which leads to sin. In all this consideration it should be noted that Jesus of Nazareth sets us a pattern for the overcoming of all temptation by His use of "It is written." Here is strength: to confront Satan with the Word of God, and use that as a shield. It is a striking thing that the One who was God Incarnate, when faced with temptation, followed the revealed Word of God. This needs to be established in the thinking of Christians today! If Jesus of Nazareth Himself, facing temptations of His human nature, followed Scripture as His defense, no one can justify using any other method of meeting the temptations Satan is constantly putting before Christians today. All personal problems can be handled in accordance with God's Word.

Once a Christian knows the revealed Word of God any attempt to solve a personal problem is not legitimate if it does not seek in the Scriptures the application of God's revelation to that problem. My Lord was tempted, and He followed the Scriptures. There can be no confidence in any person or counsellor who imagines he can find a better way to handle temptation.

It is tremendously important that Christians realize this is God's way for them. It will make a tremendous difference in their living day by day. No human being can ever know the solution for human problems. This requires the wisdom from above, as Paul knew so well when he wrote the following in I Corinthians 2:4, 5, 13:

> And my speech and my preaching was not with enticing words of man's wisdom, but in demonstration of the Spirit and of power: That your faith should not stand in the wisdom of men, but in the power of God. Which things also we speak, not in the words which man's wisdom teacheth, but which the Holy Ghost teacheth . . .

When Jesus had endured the three temptations it is written, "And when the devil had ended all the temptation, he departed from him for a season" (verse 13). For a season! Satan did not leave Jesus alone forever. As long as Jesus Christ was here on earth, He was beset by Satan who came at Him again, again, and yet again. It was as though Satan refused to accept the fact that this Jesus of Nazareth, in this body created by God for the incarnation of His Son on earth, could possibly deny entirely His natural interests in the fulfillment of the will of God.

Satan has not changed his approach, in all these years since Jesus of Nazareth walked this earth. Appealing to believers at their weakest points, appealing to them at the place where their selfishness, pride and imagination would make them most vulnerable, where they would be most susceptible to flattery, he comes seeking to dissuade believers from obeying the will of Almighty God. But Jesus of Nazareth set the pattern for the defeat of Satan: clinging to the revelation of God in His Word and will, and putting all earthly human things in second place.

Jesus and Adam

It can be helpful to compare this temptation of Jesus Christ with the temptation of Adam. Adam was tempted along these same lines. Eve saw that the tree was good for food – *appetite;* a thing pleasant to look upon – *imagination;* and something to be desired to make one wise –

vanity. When she had considered these things, she yielded and this was her sin. The temptation of Eve was not sin, but her giving in to Satan's suggestions was sin as she took and ate of the forbidden fruit. And so Adam, the first man, with all that he might desire for a happy and fruitful life, free to eat of all the trees but one, failed utterly. He failed because he followed his own ideas instead of obeying the Word of God to him.

In contrast Jesus of Nazareth, who had come as "the second Man," was not in a garden but in a desert, not surrounded with all that was lovely and good to eat, but fasting and hungry. He was tempted along these three lines and endured as victorious, not only because He was the Son of God, but because He rested utterly upon the Word of God. Thus He set this victorious example for the encouragement and strength of His followers.

This record of the temptation of Jesus of Nazareth is written for the knowledge and the guidance of all believers. Study of this scripture will reward the sincere Christian with insight into the ways of Satan, with confidence in the perfect righteousness of Jesus Christ, and with guidance in the effectual endurance of temptation. "The servant is not greater than his Master." If Jesus of Nazareth could be tempted, certainly His followers will be tempted; if Jesus could withstand the wiles of Satan every believer trusting in Christ Jesus is assured of victory in the hour of trial.

The narrative of Luke's gospel now goes on to report a number of events as they occurred in the beginning of the public ministry of Jesus of Nazareth. As pointed out above, we have no account of what He did or what happened to Him from the time He was in the temple at twelve years of age until now, when He was about thirty years of age. His first public appearance which Luke records was His baptism by John the Baptist. The next event was the temptation in the wilderness which has just been studied. After His victory in temptation He begins to minister as a teacher.

Teaching in the Synagogue (4:14-27)

Having come to His own home town, He presented Himself as Teacher in the synagogue.

> And he came to Nazareth, where he had been brought up: and, as his custom was, he went into the synagogue on the sabbath day, and stood up for to read (Luke 4:16).

This record makes one thing clear: it was the habit of Jesus of Nazareth to attend the public worship of God on the Sabbath day. In this He sets an example for every believer. Christians should be church-going people. Also, Luke reports it was His custom to participate in the proceedings of the group in their religious practices. It was His custom to take the scroll of the Scriptures, open it and read a passage therefrom. Thus on the occasion being reported:

> . . . there was delivered unto him the book of the prophet Esaias. And when he had opened the book, he found the place where it was written. The Spirit of the Lord is upon me, because he hath anointed me to preach the gospel to the poor; he hath sent me to heal the broken-hearted, to preach deliverance to the captives, and recovering of sight to the blind, to set at liberty them that are bruised, To preach the acceptable year of the Lord. And he closed the book, and he gave it again to the minister, and sat down. And the eyes of all them that were in the synagogue were fastened on him. And he began to say unto them, This day is this scripture fulfilled in your ears. And all bare him witness, and wondered at the gracious words which proceeded out of his mouth . . . (4:17-22).

Luke tells enough of the actual procedure to show it was their habit to sit down to discuss or to teach. Apparently they stood to hold the scroll while reading the Word of God, and then sat down to discuss what was written. This seems to imply they acted thus to show a reverence for the very scroll which contained the precious Word of God.

In this case Jesus of Nazareth appears to have startled the company present by telling them that the Scripture

He had just read was even that day being fulfilled before them. As He set forth His thoughts these people in His own town wondered at His grasp of the meaning of the Scriptures, and at His strong emphasis that God is gracious.

Sometimes when the Gospel is preached with emphasis upon the love of God and the grace of the Lord Jesus Christ, it may be wondered whether the truth can be so precious and so kind. Can it be really true that God will for Christ's sake receive anyone ("Whosoever will come after me," Mark 8:34) and forgive any/all sin ("Though your sins be as scarlet, they shall be as white as snow")? (Isaiah 1:18). Yet this is the promise of the Gospel! There is no limit to the call "Come unto me, all ye that labor and are heavy laden, and I will give you rest" (Matthew 11:28). There can be no greater, sweeter assurance that the words of Isaiah set forth:

> Fear thou not: for I am with thee . . . fear not, I will help thee (Isaiah 4:10,13).

The people who heard Him preach were deeply impressed with "the gracious words which proceeded out of His mouth."

And yet there were some who did not believe. Luke tells about their skepticism:

> . . . Is not this Joseph's son? And he said unto them, Ye will surely say unto me this proverb, Physician, heal thyself: whatsoever we have heard done in Capernaum, do also here in thy country. And he said, Verily I say unto you, No prophet is accepted in his own country (4:22-24).

Matthew and Mark also tell of this incident that when Jesus began teaching and preaching in His own country, performing miracles to win their confidence, His neighbors gathered around skeptically. They thought of Him in His human nature, and naturally questioned His authority. It was almost as if they were saying: "Who does this

young man think he is? He grew up in our midst. Let
him show us something, let him convince us of his power."

What happened in that instance makes it plain that
when any man or woman comes to God in a skeptical
frame of mind, nothing great will happen. Almighty God
will not show off His power and glory, as in a circus pa-
rade. He will not do His wonderful works to satisfy the
cavilling doubts of unwilling skeptics. It will disqualify
anyone to approach Almighty God in such a fashion. This
is very similar to what happened at the crucifixion:

> And they that passed by reviled him, wagging their heads,
> And saying, Thou that destroyest the temple, and buildest
> it in three days, save thyself. If thou be the Son of God,
> come down from the cross. Likewise also the chief priests
> mocking him, with the scribes and elders, said, He saved
> others; himself he cannot save. If he be the King of Israel,
> let him now come down from the cross, and we will believe
> him (Matthew 27:39-42).

There was no answer then, only a great silence from
heaven. The suffering Saviour on the cross uttered no
word. It is possible those foolish people could arrive at
a superficial judgment saying: "We gave Him an opportunity. We gave Him a chance but He could offer no
proof." Such would be the talk of fools, and for such
idle words men will be held accountable in the Day of
Judgment.

On this occasion when He was so challenged by His
neighbor, Matthew reports, "And he did not many mighty
works there because of their unbelief" (Matthew 13:58).
Mark's comment tells more:

> And he could there do no mighty work, save that he laid
> his hands upon a few sick folk, and healed them. And he
> marvelled because of their unbelief . . . (Mark 6:5, 6).

What a sad commentary on that group of people!
Even today it is possible for men and women to have a
similar skepticism in a frame of mind that would seek
to reduce Jesus Christ to being merely human. This will

help to explain how it is possible for a group to use His Name, to hear about Him in the Gospel, and yet see no results, because of such unbelief in the hearts of those who listen. Emphasizing this human nature of Jesus Christ will hinder God from doing any mighty work among them. Jesus comments upon this:

> But I tell you of a truth, many widows were in Israel in the days of Elias, when the heaven was shut up three years and six months, when great famine was throughout all the land; But unto none of them was Elias sent, save unto Sarepta, a city of Sidon, unto a woman that was a widow. And many lepers were in Israel in the time of Eliseus the prophet; and none of them was cleansed, saving Naaman the Syrian (Luke 4:25-27).

When the people in the local synagogue realized He was exposing their unbelief they were filled with anger. They felt His choice of Old Testament incidents was a reflection upon them. The widow of Sarepta was the one who took the last bit of meal she had and made a cake of it for Elijah the prophet at his request. She believed God, and gave what she had in obedient response to His will. Naaman the Syrian, against his own inclination, against his own pride, did what Elisha the prophet told him: he went and bathed himself seven times in the river Jordan, even though he felt foolish and was deeply humiliated by such action. But his leprosy was healed! The implication is plain. If the word of the prophet had not been obeyed, healing would never have come, and so his neighbors felt He was threatening them for their fortunate response to His preaching.

The Lord Jesus was saying plainly to these people in His home town that they were having their opportunity, but if they did not obey, there would be no blessing. Such plain talk was not at all appreciated. They were

> . . . filled with wrath, And rose up, and thrust him out of the city, and led him unto the brow of the hill whereon their city was built, that they might cast him down headlong. But he passing through the midst of them went his way (4:28-30).

How Did Jesus Escape? (4:28-32)

There is no description of the Lord's actions in this incident. There is no word as to how He did what was done. I have often had many ideas as I have read the New Testament about things which are not set forth in detail, as I try to understand what happened. In this case I have the impression that Jesus turned and looked at the crowd as they were about to destroy Him. I have often wished I might have seen that look. I am reminded of the soldiers who came to arrest Him in the Garden of Gethsemane. When He turned and asked whom they were seeking, they fell on their faces, ran away, and had to come back a second time. I have the feeling that as this group of angry people brought him to the brow of that high hill and would have thrown Him down, He turned and looked at them with the look that may have been similar to the manner in which He looked at those men who wanted to stone the woman taken in adultery. In that case when they brought the accused woman before Him, they quoted the law of Moses to Him, trying to tempt Him, so that they might have something to accuse Him. The record reads:

> . . . But Jesus stooped down, and with his finger wrote on the ground, as though he heard them not. So when they continued asking him, he lifted up himself, and said unto them, He that is without sin among you, let him first cast a stone at her. And again he stooped down, and wrote on the ground (John 8:6-8).

There is always something majestic, something awe-inspiring about simple, naked truth. No one could face His challenge. All went out leaving Him alone with the woman. In some such way He may have quietly turned and looked at those who would have destroyed Him over the edge of that cliff and then simply passed by them and went His way!

An Unclean Spirit Cast Out (4:33-37)

After this Jesus came to Capernaum, a city of Galilee, and on the Sabbath He began to teach in their synagogue.

> And in the synagogue there was a man, which had a spirit of an unclean devil, and cried out with a loud voice, Saying, Let us alone; what have we to do with thee, thou Jesus of Nazareth? Art thou come to destroy us? I know thee who thou art; the Holy One of God. And Jesus rebuked him, saying, Hold thy peace, and come out of him. And when the devil had thrown him in the midst, he came out of him, and hurt him not. And they were all amazed, and spake among themselves, saying, What a word is this! for with authority and power he commandeth the unclean spirits, and they come out. And the fame of him went out into every place of the country round about (Luke 4:33-37).

This reflects something tragic! The neighbors did not recognize the Son of God, but the devil did! The unclean spirit knew who this was who commanded him to come out, and he obeyed. Oh! the sad fact that many who have heard of Him in His human form do not *know* who He really is! In the earthly ministry of Jesus of Nazareth from time to time He demonstrated the authority and power which He had as the Son of God. Thus He showed His control over nature, over natural factors and forces, so that people seeing the evidence marveled at the powers of His word, His amazing authority. It was so at this time and fame of Him went abroad like wildfire so that people began to gather around Him.

Luke reports:

> . . . he arose out of the synagogue, and entered into Simon's house. And Simon's wife's mother was taken with a great fever; and they besought him for her. And he stood over her, and rebuked the fever; and it left her; and immediately she arose and ministered unto them (4:38,39).

In the course of His wonderful works the power of Jesus of Nazareth was demonstrated over sickness, with the result that people from all around the area began to bring their sick folk to Him. The record is clear: he laid his hands on them, and healed them. Demons also came out of many, crying out, and saying, "Thou art Christ the Son of God." Luke records that He "rebuking them suffered them not to speak: for they knew that he was Christ."

At this point Jesus departed into a desert place. It is possible He sought rest and communion with His Father. But the people continued to seek Him. They came to Him and insisted upon delaying Him, "that he should not depart from them. And he said unto them, I must preach the kingdom of God to other cities also: for therefore am I sent. And he preached in the synagogues of Galilee" (4:42-44).

JESUS' PREACHING (5:1-3)

Chapter five continues the same story, " . . . the people pressed upon him . . . to hear the word of God" (verse 1). When Jesus of Nazareth preached the Word of God, what did He say? Perhaps the answer is to be found as one looks at the Sermon on the Mount, as it is called, in Matthew 5-7. Then one should look at the parables He taught in the thirteenth chapter of Matthew, and at other reports of His teaching. It is quite probable that Jesus was doing the same kind of preaching that John the Baptist did, using the same general theme: *Repent and believe! The kingdom of God is at hand!* No doubt Jesus would make clear that Almighty God, who gave His law to Moses and who inspired the prophets in the Old Testament, was really and truly God, and that Israel would have to deal with Him in terms of the revealed, eternal law of God.

No doubt this was the kind of preaching Jesus of Nazareth did; but over and above that, He showed something that Moses and the others never had. As He taught and preached He exercised the power to deliver and to save anyone who would come to Him.

At the time when Jesus of Nazareth came there had been generations of Jewish teaching. The prophets had preached, and after the prophets the scribes had come teaching, so that the people had been well-informed as to what the Bible – that is, the Old Testament – said. The Scriptures had been interpreted to them. In the Talmud rabbis had stated their opinion as to what the law meant, such as would be available today in commentaries on the Bible. The Jews had this material, helpful for better understanding, even though at times it came short of the whole truth. These rabbis gave their understanding about the meaning of the Scripture as they taught, but it was not possible for them to know the grace of God which was later revealed in Jesus Christ. Thus when Jesus was teaching, time and time again He would say, "Your rabbis have been saying this, but I tell you from the beginning it was not so." Then He would quote exactly the Old Testament Scripture, and show what those words really meant. Even so He could not tell them all they would one day know since He had not yet died and been raised from the dead (John 13:7 and 16:12).

This is the explanation of His command when He sent His disciples out, two by two, and told them not to go to the Gentiles, but to go only to the House of Israel. At that time they did not yet have the Gospel to preach, the Gospel that is now preached to the whole world. The fact was that Jesus of Nazareth had not yet died: He had not yet paid the penalty for sin, nor had He been raised from the dead in glorious victory and triumph over sin. They could not yet point to the sacrifice of Jesus Christ, for they did not yet know about it themselves. They could only point back to the Old Testament types and figures and patterns, and say, This is what God has promised and will do. They could present the law of God and teach it, saying in clear terms what the holiness of God demands. It is only in the death of Jesus Christ for sinners and in the power of His Resurrection that the saving grace of God can be seen. The message of the demands of the law and the call to repentance could be understood from the Scriptures by the people who had the Old Testament, namely Israel.

A Leper Cleansed (5:12-14)

Luke then goes on to tell about the man

. . . full of leprosy: who seeing Jesus fell on his face, and besought him, saying, Lord, if thou wilt, thou canst make me clean. And he put forth his hand, and touched him, saying, I will: be thou clean. And immediately the leprosy departed from him (5:12, 13).

This man no doubt was aware of the common view that leprosy was incurable. But there had come to him a challenging hope because of Jesus of Nazareth. He gave expression to what was in his heart as he cried: "Lord, if Thou wilt, thou canst make me clean." This miracle is so very significant to all men. It makes no difference what burden a man or woman may bring to the Lord. It cannot possibly be anything worse than leprosy. If one should come, feeling down deep in his or her heart: "I am unclean, I am personally unfit to approach a holy God," such an one can be assured, "Come, as you are, He is all you can need in all the world. Look at Him." He *could,* if He *would?* He can and He will do it. The leper came and was cleansed. The record goes on with the simple report: " . . . the leprosy departed from him." The Lord with the healing touch is just the same today. This is what authorizes the preaching of His saving power with all confidence. He did it then and He can do it now.

A Time for Prayer (5:16)

In a short simple statement Luke now reports a most significant action on the part of Jesus of Nazareth: "And he withdrew himself into the wilderness, and prayed."

This is an amazing thing! This Person who had accomplished so many wonderful things so early in His public ministry: who had cast out the unclean spirit, healed Simon's wife's mother, laid His hands on a multitude of sick folk, healing them, demonstrated His power over the fish in the sea, cleansed the leper with just a word, in the full demonstration of His power: this Jesus of Nazareth withdrew Himself from all of them, and went out into the country alone! Why? Apparently to commune with His Father God. What a profound example for His followers.

This seems to point out a very important lesson. If God has just done some great favor for any person, lifted a burden, touched the heart, forgiven sin and made that one whole, opened up the way where before all had looked dark and gloomy so that now the heart is filled with joy and elation – then such an one should take the time to get away from people, even from people who may praise God for what has happened, especially from people who would look upon him with adulation, to a quiet place, where that soul can be alone with God the Father. Now is the time to get straightened out in thinking. It could be that a rush of emotion, even of the exaltation that comes from the touch of God upon the heart, could confuse such a person for a time. The great things which have happened have come to pass for the glory of God and should be so recognized. The believer is just a humble human being, fortunate in having such a Lord who has done such wonderful things. The living Lord will draw that soul to Himself, if that person will come apart and seek His face. It is far, far better to be close to the Lord than to be prominent, notable, amazing or astonishing to others at a time when God does great things for a person and through that person to the glory of His Name.

At a time when anyone has been greatly blessed it is important to thank the Lord for what He has done, praise His Holy Name for every benefit received, and to take time to be alone with Him. It is always more important to have communion with God than to have the praise of men. This may well be what Jesus found when He sought quiet communion with His Father. So will any blessed soul find it, with joy and peace never known before! It is for the fortunate believer to trust God, believe in His Word, and yield everything else into His loving care!

Chapter 5

THE MIRACLES OF CHRIST

In the gospel of Luke it is not so much the story of the events that happened that is important, as it is the description of Jesus of Nazareth in what He did and what happened to Him. It may seem strange to point out that what Jesus did, and suffered, and taught cannot by itself save the soul. For if this were possible then all men would be saved, since Christ Jesus certainly died for the sins of the whole world, and "God is no respecter of persons." But the truth is that "whosoever shall call upon the name of the Lord shall be saved." "As many as received him, to them gave he power to become the children of God." Since salvation is by faith, it is essential that the soul believe in Jesus Christ.

RECEIVING FAITH

Faith must be given to the soul. Faith is not natural. "Faith cometh by hearing, and hearing by the word of God" (Romans 10:17). Faith is not something a person can make up out of his own mind: that would be "make believe." Nor is faith merely pious intention of the soul. Luke told Theophilus he had written his gospel so that his friend "mightest know the certainty of those things, wherein thou hast been instructed." But believing in the Lord Jesus Christ means much more than simply accepting as true and accurate the records of what happened. Saving faith is grounded in the heartfelt conviction that Jesus was and is the Christ, the Son of the living God. To generate such faith, the gospels were written to show the truth as to who Jesus of Nazareth really was. This was done by reporting certain things He did and certain things He said (John 20:30, 31).

Believing as an exercise of the soul cannot save in itself. It is believing the promises of God in Christ that saves the soul. Believing is like swallowing. While it could be said a person lives by swallowing, this would not actually be an adequate statement. It is by swallowing food the body lives: a person could swallow poison and die. Even so in the matter of believing. Believing error will lead to destruction. Believing nothing will leave a man in his sins. It is believing the truth about Jesus Christ that saves the soul.

Believing in God is a short way of saying that you believe in God whom Jesus Christ revealed and that you believe in what He said He would do. Jesus offered Himself as the Saviour and Lord, saying that whosoever will believe in Him should not perish, but should have everlasting life. But who is He? The truth about Him was shown in His public ministry, and is recorded in the four gospels. Thus, Jesus came to show the Word of God, to show the promises of God, so that people could know the truth in these words. Yet just knowing the words as such is not enough. Even today in teaching, words are used, but teachers also use illustrations. Preachers use all manner of descriptions, figures of speech, and examples from human experience in which other people have walked with God, in order to convey the meaning of what is being said in so many words.

When a person is going to believe, he will need to believe with the understanding. He doesn't have to know everything when he first comes to God, but he must know and accept Jesus Christ. Knowing how to spell the name of Jesus is not knowing Him. Knowing that He lived and died is not yet knowing Him. It is when man comes to realize that Jesus Christ came for him and died for him so that he puts his trust in Him, then there is the beginning of God's working in that soul. The witness of the fruits of the Holy Spirit at work in the soul will be

seen when that man testifies with joy that God is working in him to will and to do of His good pleasure. It is
then that the Christian can give a confident testimony
to the whole world.

> This poor man cried, and the Lord heard him, and saved
> him out of all his troubles (Psalm 34:6).

God sent the Lord Jesus Christ to show men what
He, the Father, was like. The Lord Jesus said, " . . . he
that hath seen me hath seen the Father . . ." (John 14:9).
This did not refer to His physical appearance. It is the
record of what Jesus did, as set forth in Matthew, Mark,
Luke and John, with the significance which the Old Testament Scriptures reveal about these events, which shows
Jesus of Nazareth to be the Christ who was promised as
the Saviour. When any soul believes in Him as the Christ,
he will be saved by the power of God.

When Jesus of Nazareth was teaching, He was showing primarily how God does things. He drew illustrations
from nature, but He never took time to teach about nature
as is done in the natural sciences. He took examples
from the lives and actions of men and women, but He
did not teach about human nature as is done in the social
sciences. He was teaching, first and last, about God.
This was what He alone could teach. Since He *was* the
only begotten Son of God, He could truly demonstrate
to the people of His day the actions of God, inviting
people to trust Him. He could in effect say to them:
"Trust Me, and in trusting Me, you are trusting God.
Take My word, and you are taking God's Word. Believe
in Me: you believe in the Father, believe in Me also."
This was the burden of His teaching. This was how He
presented Himself to men then; and He still does today.

THE RESURRECTION OF THE DEAD

The greatest single promise in the Gospel is that God
will raise the dead. Death is the common lot of all: not

only physically but socially and spiritually man is dying
and deteriorating. Despite energetic efforts in education,
culture and civilization, in which man has achieved some
postponement, the terminal prospect is unchanged. Even
"the paths of glory lead but to the grave." Man is doomed
to die and to decay in death. But God can in Jesus Christ
raise the dead into newness of life. The great work of
resurrection from the dead will be done by the power
of God in Jesus Christ.

When Jesus of Nazareth taught that God can and will
work wonders by His power He did not claim such results
would be the work of natural factors and processes. He
always made it clear that God's power would be shown
in the resurrection from the dead. This is the power that
created man in the world originally, and has kept him
throughout all existence. It is the mighty power of God
by which He raised Jesus of Nazareth from the dead which
is the ground for the confidence of the believer that he
too shall be raised from the dead.

Human beings are not strong enough nor good enough
to face the issues of eternity and God. Man is a sinner:
he is facing doom, and all men feel the shadow of this
impending destruction. But into that gloom comes the
bright and morning star of the grace of God in the Gospel
of Jesus Christ. Jesus said to Martha,

> I am the resurrection, and the life: he that believeth in
> me, though he were dead, yet shall he live: And whoso-
> ever liveth and believeth in me shall never die . . . (John
> 11:25, 26).

Through His Resurrection Christ can bring victory over
all that is now threatening man. "Wherefore he is able
to save them to the uttermost that come unto God by
him, seeing he ever liveth to make intercession for them"
(Hebrews 7:25). This is the gracious message of the Gospel
of Christ. "Whosoever believeth in him should not perish,
but have eternal life" (John 3:16).

Salvation is promised in the Gospel to all who believe

in their hearts that God raised Jesus Christ from the dead
(Romans 10:9). But how can a man believe that God could
or would raise the dead? This was difficult for the disciples to believe even when Jesus Himself stood before
them in His resurrection body (Luke 24:36-43). It would
be quite impossible for the people with whom Jesus of
Nazareth was dealing to believe in such promises of God
without being shown some demonstration of the power
of God. Here can be seen a very practical reason for the
miracles which Jesus performed. In order to show the intention and the power of God to raise the dead, and to
show that He was the Son of God to whom the Father
gave this power, Jesus performed miracles to the astonishment of all who saw and heard Him (Luke 5:17-26). By
such wonderful works of power He demonstrated God's
control over the natural processes, and prepared the hearts
of men to be able to believe in the resurrection of the
dead.

The people among whom Jesus of Nazareth lived understood the things of nature. The earth, the sea, the sun,
the rain, the winds surrounded them. Every day they
could see that fortune and welfare were involved as man
manipulated the natural processes. "Whatsoever a man
soweth, that shall he also reap" was common knowledge
to them all. And they knew that in the natural process
death was the end of every living thing: "The grass wither-
eth, the flower fadeth" was in common experience.

At the same time they knew that within certain limitations man could manipulate nature to his advantage.
Man was "to subdue the earth and have dominion over
it." They could understand that benefits could be secured
by intelligent control. But they knew also that man's
power is limited. Man can control some natural events
but only God could control all. They understood that God
was almighty: that nothing was impossible with God.
Man could not overcome death. Only God could raise
the dead. But would this be the will of God? Should
they believe that God would control nature, and over-

come natural processes for their benefit?

In the teaching of the Scriptures the Jews had learned much about God. God is everywhere. God is not the product of the natural world. God is Himself the Creator of the heavens and the earth, and of man, and as Almighty God, single and solitary in His holiness and grandeur, He watches over His creation. He made man in His own image, but He is apart from man, for He is God, " . . . the King eternal, immortal, invisible, the only wise God . . . " (I Timothy 1:17). "In Him we live, and move, and have our being" (Acts 17:28). Man's spiritual welfare involves his personal relationship with the Judge of all the earth; it includes his personal living forever by God's grace and power in what is called *eternal life.* It includes the prospect of heaven. It includes God's daily ministration of grace to the soul. Everything meant by the words *spiritual welfare* is directly involved in man's believing response in obeying God.

THE MESSAGE OF THE MIRACLES

Jesus of Nazareth came to show that man can have dealings with God. In order that men might know, Jesus taught and demonstrated. He did certain things that were miraculous to the astonishment of the people around Him. Then He interpreted what He had done. He taught them what His actions meant. It was in order to demonstrate God's power to rule over the natural processes and to overrule natural events, as well as to show His own credentials as the Son of God, that Jesus worked miracles. He actually manipulated natural processes to work wonders with them, such as no one but God could have done. By way of illustration, Luke 6:17-19 stresses this:

> And he came down with them, and stood in the plain, and the company of his disciples, and a great multitude of people out of all Judaea and Jerusalem, and from the sea coast of Tyre and Sidon, which came to hear him, and to be healed of their diseases: And they that were

vexed with unclean spirits: and they were healed. And
the whole multitude sought to touch him: for there went
virtue out of him, and healed them all.

Men are acquainted with many natural processes in
this world. There are laws of nature which involve sickness; storms that damage; illness that brings death; and
many such things which follow in natural sequence. One
thing leads to another, and then to another and thus on
to difficulty or distress, bringing sorrow and pain. Jesus
worked miracles to reveal there is Someone above this
world, in and through this world, in final control of the
natural order, and this was His Father, the Lord God
Almighty.

Control Over Disease

As Jesus of Nazareth found men in need He overruled
natural processes, controlling these in what we call
miracles, but He also did more than that. In the case of
the leper who came to Him for help, Jesus did more than
heal him. One important aspect of this healing of the
leper is to be seen in considering the fact that in that
day lepers were expected to keep away from other people
They were to cry out "Unclean! Unclean!" when anyone
came near them. This was the law, and all lepers lived
under this quarantine or imposed social control, because
leprosy was considered to be a highly communicable disease. But when this leper came to Jesus, He touched
him (Luke 5:13). No Jew would dream of touching a
leper, no matter how sad or painful the poor man's physical condition. But Jesus touched the leper, telling him to
be clean. And instantly the leprosy was cleansed, taken
away. This was astonishing! He had acted in a way that
was contrary to the Jewish laws for safeguarding the people from this dread disease, as well as contrary to physical
laws, for at that time there was no known cure for leprosy. He was preparing them to understand that God can
do beyond natural processes and will do more than man
can think.

Control Over Elements

Jesus also demonstrated control over the elements of nature. On one occasion as he was sailing across the lake, having fallen asleep in the boat, a furious windstorm threatened to sink the ship. The disciples wakened Him, asking for help. "Then he arose, and rebuked the wind and the raging of the water: and they ceased, and there was a calm" (Luke 8:24). Such control over nature was astonishing even to His disciples, but there was never any doubt as to the meaning of this incident: Jesus of Nazareth was someone extraordinary!

Power Over Creatures

There were other miracles which pointed to the same truth. Such was the incident when Jesus performed the miracle of the tremendous draught of fishes. This was another demonstration of His power over the creatures as well as the elements of this world. Then there was the man sick of the palsy, to whom Jesus said, "Thy sins be forgiven thee." Immediately people murmured and asked how He could forgive sins,

> And Jesus knowing their thoughts said, Wherefore think ye evil in your hearts? For whether is easier, to say, Thy sins be forgiven thee; or to say, Arise, and walk? But that ye may know that the Son of man hath power on earth to forgive sins, (then saith he to the sick of the palsy,) Arise, take up thy bed, and go unto thine house. And he arose, and departed to his house (Matthew 9:4-7).

Only God could do that! So this healing was a demonstration of the limitless power of God, for only God could set a man free from sin.

Also there were miracles in which He showed authority over the power of demons, and then again over the final enemy, death. In these amazing demonstrations Jesus of Nazareth showed His power as the Son of God.

The Scope of the Miracles

The question might well be asked why did Jesus do such miracles? Did He intend to free all men from leprosy? Would He set Himself up as a healer to help all blind men and women? Apparently not, and yet the miracles seemed to serve some purpose. Amazing as they were, the miracles Jesus performed were incidental to His chief purpose. He came to deal with individuals themselves, that He might bring them into right relationship with God. He wanted men to know God, that they might realize what God could do. He wanted them to know that God *would* show His love for them. Jesus of Nazareth was not interested in improving this world as an eternal habitation. But He used instances of human need in this world to demonstrate the truth and the blessing of eternal life, in order that human beings might accept this gift of the Father here and now, and then enjoy it forever.

A further significance might be seen in the miracles. It is important to note that all Jesus needed to do in each instance was to speak the word of authority, and things happened: waves were stilled, men were healed, lepers were cleansed, dead men rose. Even in the case of the man whose blind eyes were anointed with clay, there was no medical or healing virtue in the clay. It was the word of Jesus which restored the sight.

It seems clear that these wonders which the Lord Jesus worked were the manipulation of natural events and phenomena by the Word of God at His will. When Jesus spoke things happened in the natural world. This could imply that the Word of God written in the Scriptures today has power, just as the living Word incarnate in Jesus of Nazareth had power. Every saved man and woman today knows that the Word of God has power to change human beings in his will, in his heart. Jesus was in human form Himself when these miracles were worked, and He used these wonders to show the power and love of God. Yet it is not unreasonable to conclude that the Lord Jesus Christ who now is in the presence of God the Father is working by His Spirit. The miracles of the earthly career of Jesus of Nazareth and the miracles of the present ministry of Christ at the right hand of the Father alike show the power of God.

Something of the significance of the miracles can be seen in a simple illustration. Suppose a person wanted to confer with the manager of some huge electric power installation. He came to the plant for such an interview. Suppose he met a man clad in workman's clothes to whom he made his request that he might see the manager. The workman claimed to be the manager, though his appearance was much more humble than might have been expected. How could this worker have overcome the natural skepticism of the visitor? Suppose he stepped to a control switch and by pulling it stopped the huge dynamos, and then again started the machinery. Suppose this were done a number of times with no interference from anyone else in the plant. Would this not be convincing proof that he was indeed the one in control? When Jesus of Nazareth manipulated natural processes at His will by His Word, He was demonstrating that He was indeed the Son of God, acting under authority from His Father.

The question might arise as to the rarity of miracles. Why do they not happen more frequently? Reflection could help to see that the frequent occurrence of interruption in the natural course of events could be very unsettling to the minds of men. Constancy of process and consistency in performance enables man to have confidence and to feel at peace. If you should sit on a chair, you expect that chair to be solid. If it should suddenly be as foam rubber when it was believed to be oak, you would be naturally upset. If this were to happen several times without warning you could suffer actual mental imbalance. The sanity of men depends upon the stability of such elements in the environment as are taken to be known and sure. Thus it is the benevolent mercy of God to sustain natural processes and affairs in reliable consistency. The very operation of scientific research depends upon the constancy of natural elements. Just so the intelligence of man is dependent upon a consistent uniformity in the course of affairs. "Whatsoever a man soweth that shall he also reap" is absolutely essential to any understanding or to any system of values or ethics. Any miracles would be a startling shock as it was in the days of Jesus of Nazareth. He employed miracles only because of the great importance of the truth He was showing to men.

Jesus of Nazareth wanted to help men to receive Him as the Son of God, and to believe in the resurrection of the dead. How could Jesus identify Himself to the people of His day? They did not know what God looked like. Jesus looked like a man, coming in the form of a servant, made in the flesh. How could He then gain the confidence of people, bringing them to the point of faith in Him as God, unless He acted as God? And this He did! He multiplied a few fishes to feed five thousand. This is why it is so important to accept the miracle as it is written, for only so is it possible truly to know the God of the Bible. The God of the Bible is the God who can manipulate natural processes to suit His own ends. If anyone should exclaim that he never saw anything like it, this would of course be true. No one has ever seen anything like what God can and will do through His Son Jesus Christ.

If anyone should see a person doing what Jesus of Nazareth did: opening the eyes of the blind; enabling a dumb man to speak; causing a lame man to walk; restoring withered arms; lifting a paralyzed man and making him walk; even raising the dead, surely the impression would be, *this must be God at work!* And this is exactly the way it worked out for Jesus. When Nicodemus came to interview Him, he said:

. . . Rabbi, we know that thou art a teacher come from God: for no man can do these miracles that thou doest, except God be with him (John 3:2).

THE MIRACLE OF SALVATION

Believers should always keep in mind that if salvation ever takes place, it will be because they believe God did raise Jesus of Nazareth and that He can raise the dead. That is the biggest miracle that can ever happen. In the same way the greatest truth about God which the Lord Jesus Christ wanted to make known to every believer is that God can, by His power, raise a believer from the dead *spiritually,* and make a new person out of him. God will also raise his physical body one day, but that lies in the future. Every person in Christ Jesus becomes a new creature, as Paul has told us in II Corinthians 5:17:

> Therefore if any man be in Christ, he is a new creature: old things are passed away; behold, all things are become new.

This miracle of regeneration, the greatest of all, happens day by day all over the world by the power of God: the same power which He manifested when He raised up Jesus Christ from the dead: the same power which Jesus of Nazareth demonstrated when He worked these miracles in the days of His flesh.

Another observation that can be noted about the miracles is that they seem always to be practical and helpful in their effect upon the persons involved. There is an element of intelligence about them which can easily be overlooked because of the startling impact of the miraculous aspect in each case. The miracle can be seen as indicating the purpose of God in restoring to normalcy, delivering from affliction and saving from distress. Something of this is to be seen in each miracle, as well as often they correct the consequence of sin. Whatever needed healing or restoration in the people upon whom Jesus performed His miracles was the result of sin. Thus there seems to be a very real revelation of the plan of God in the miracles, in that they can be seen as examples of the total

work of deliverance and restoration which God intends
to achieve through Jesus Christ.

The problem of how Christ's will could affect natural
phenomena suggests the problem of how man's will can
affect the actions of his body. Consider the hand of a
man. It is related to the rest of his body in a physiological
way. But what makes the hand close or open? What makes
the hand rise or fall? To be sure muscles and nerves are
involved in these acts, but what stimulates the nerves?
What directs the muscles? Modern science of man seems
not to be clear in its understanding, but the popular
opinion is that it is the *will* of man. No matter how it
is psychologically described a man feels the reason why
his hand lifts is because *he lifts it:* it lowers because he
lowers it. A man feels his fist clench because he *clenches
it:* it will open because *he opens the fingers.* Every instance of motion is because the man wills it. A man is
in his body but he is not the body. The body is his
house, and he dwells in it. There is a person inside every
human body. That person leaves the body at death. In
fact it is that person whom his friends really love.

A baby may weigh seven pounds, six ounces at birth.
Later that body may weigh 176 pounds. But the soul
does not grow in that fashion. The person inhabiting
that body is not involved in that weight gain. The little
baby boy was named John and throughout his life those
who live with him will still call him John. He may live
to be a hundred, but he will always be John. He is John
all the time, a certain person with whom others have to
deal. When he dies, John's body will be laid in a grave,
but John will not be in that grave. To the comfort and
joy of the Christian, the body of the loved ones may be
put in the grave, but the *person* will be with Christ. Believers are separated from loved ones for only a little
while, until the Lord comes. Soul and body will be re-
united in the resurrection, and loved ones will be together
"forever with the Lord." That is the Christian's hope about
death, lifting bereaved hearts out of despair and loneliness

when a loved one dies. The earthly tabernacle may return to the earth in the death of the body, but the soul goes on to be with the Lord.

The relationship of the soul to the body can be seen as similar to the relationship of the invisible, spiritual God to the universe which He created. Throughout Scripture God is revealed as transcendent over, and yet present in, His creation, moving at will, accomplishing His work as He wishes. Man was created in the image of God, and something of this likeness may be seen in that man was given dominion over the earth (Genesis 1:26,28). Man was to till the soil and make the earth bring forth to supply man with all his needs. This reveals something of the nature of man, and it is possible that this dominion of man over the earth is still seen in the control a man has over his body. However, unlike God, a person does not have total dominion over himself. When the body gets sick, the person cannot completely control it. The body may have aches and pains that the person cannot stop. It may have weaknesses, and nothing the person can do can overcome them. The body will deteriorate as the years go by, and the person cannot stop that process. A cancer may begin, and the person may not be able to check its growth. When the body is healthy, it is normal for the person to be able to move and act, using his body as he will.

When Jesus worked His miracles, it may be the whole significance was not only to show that Jesus was the Son of God, but also to show the possibilities of man when God is in him and working through him. The Son of God was in a human form, in which God dwelt. He was God incarnate in the flesh. Thus the miracles signify not only that Jesus was the Son of God, but they imply the possibilities of man when he is in full fellowship with God. They may also show that the purpose of Christ's redeeming work is to bring man into such relationship.

Throughout this discussion of the miracles which Luke records in his account it has been clearly felt that Jesus had a deliberate purpose in performing these wonders before the people of His day. He was teaching about His Father and preparing souls to believe in Him and in His promise to raise the dead. Thus the miracles are an essential part of the record written as "a declaration of those things which are most surely believed among us," and need to be taken as they are written that men may "know the certainty of those things, wherein thou hast been instructed" (Luke 1:1, 4).

Chapter 6

THE TEACHING METHODS OF
JESUS OF NAZARETH

Jesus of Nazareth spent much time in teaching and preaching. Hours of patient discussion and instruction were presented to correct natural errors in thinking about God and to develop a true understanding of what man can and should do that he might have the blessing of God. Luke could not possibly give a complete report of all that Jesus "began to do and to teach," but he has recorded enough to give a true account of the subjects discussed, the manner of teaching and the contents utilized by Jesus of Nazareth as He went about teaching the people.

John the Baptist had been preaching with sensational effectiveness before Jesus of Nazareth made His public appearance. When Jesus presented Himself to be baptized John openly endorsed Him as the Christ, as the Lamb of God, and encouraged his own disciples to follow Jesus rather than himself.

Preaching the Kingdom

Jesus began to preach shortly after His baptism and He used the same text as John had used: "Repent: for the kingdom of heaven is at hand" (Matthew 4:17). This call to repentance is a direct call to turn away from self and to turn to God. People apart from God may be doing the best they can, working through life as well as they know how, but that is not good enough. Jesus did not show them a better way to work. He did not show them better or wiser methods, or exhort and admonish them to try harder. He took into account that men had failed, that they had no strength of their own and so would fail again. God's wonderful plan in the Gospel was to substitute Christ for them, so they would live their lives through His power, not their own. When this work of God is accomplished through the message of the Gospel by it being accepted by the individual human being, it becomes "Christ in you, the hope of glory" (Colossians 1:27). But such transformation cannot take place without the Gospel being understood as it is being believed. To enable men to understand Jesus took time to teach.

Both John the Baptist and Jesus of Nazareth preached and taught for the same reason: that men might know how to receive the blessing of God as set forth in His promises. What is this blessing of God? If the Lord Jesus came to preach the kingdom of God, what difference would it make? If a man entered into the kingdom of God, what kind of an experience would he have? Certain promises of God will show what would follow:

> And I will walk among you, and will be your God, and ye shall be my people (Leviticus 26:12).

> . . . God hath said, I will dwell in them, and walk in them; and I will be their God, and they shall be my people. Wherefore come out from among them, and be ye separate, saith the Lord, and touch not the unclean thing; and I will receive you. And will be a Father unto you, and ye shall be my sons and daughters, saith the Lord Almighty (II Corinthians 6:16-18).

This, then, is the end result toward which the whole revelation of Scripture points. This is the goal toward which Jesus Christ preached, calling men to come to God, showing them how to trust God, making it clear that by trusting Him they might come into this relationship with Him. The final result for them is found in Matthew 11:28-30:

> Come unto me, all ye that labour and are heavy laden, and I will give you rest. Take my yoke upon you, and learn of me; for I am meek and lowly in heart: and ye shall find rest unto your souls. For my yoke is easy, and my burden is light.

eace is a wonderful prospect for the human heart.
yone would want to be at rest and at peace. This is
mised together with joy, inward satisfaction, and con-
entment for those who believe in God and trust in Him.
This is the *blessing of God.*

Such a wonderful prospect raises another question:
why do not more people take advantage of such blessing?
The answer to that can be given in one small, three-
letter word – *sin.* Deep down in every human heart is the
disposition to be sinful. Sometimes man is simply per-
verse, crooked: turned from the right condition, alienated
from God. The road may lie straight ahead plainly enough:
man will turn to the right or to the left. Here may be
the way to God, spread openly in plain sight; but human
hearts will wander away from Him, tending to lean in
any other direction rather than into the presence of God
in heaven.

The basic reason is sin, the inward disposition of man
to seek his own way, and to do what he wants to do rather
than what God wants. Involved in this is guilt in varying
degrees. Man hates to come before God because he feels
guilty when he approaches His presence. Sin separates
a man from God, alienates and isolates him from God.
Trying to live in and by himself with weakness of will
and blemish of character as the result of sin, matters get
worse and worse. At this point the question is even more
critical: how can a man *ever* be blessed by God? God may
be willing to give peace and rest, but how can He ever
do it?

It is important to remember that salvation is the way,
and this is what the Son of God came to bring. Salvation
embraces all that Jesus of Nazareth preached and taught.
Jesus showed that it is God who works, who saves; and
the sinner must place trust and confidence in Him. A
man needs to believe in God; he needs to commit himself to Him and receive from Him what He wants to
give. Thus will the promise of God be activated in the

believer, enabling him to realize the will of God in his life.

Faith, as has been noted above, is generated within the heart, where it is begotten by the Word of God and nurtured by that unchanging Word. Peter expressed it when he wrote: "As newborn babes, desire the sincere milk of the word, that ye may grow thereby" (I Peter 2:2).

Faith in the Christian needs to grow, and it will grow by constant feeding on the Word of God. Faith is produced and nurtured by teaching of the Word. "So then faith cometh by hearing, and hearing by the word of God" (Romans 10:17).

Luke reports that Jesus of Nazareth, while He was here during His three years of public ministry, went about preaching the "glad tidings of the kingdom of God." This says plainly that the preaching of the Gospel should bring to the human soul something properly called *glad tidings.* If preaching only showed man something else to try, something better to do than his efforts thus far, it would not be glad tidings. It is possible many people stay away from church, turn away from God and from Gospel preaching, fail to read their Bibles or look to God at all, because they feel they have done the best they could and have failed, so there is no hope left for them. What such people need to hear is the glad tidings of the Gospel of the kingdom of God, in His loving provision for every need of sinful man.

The truth of the kingdom of God is such that a sinner can rejoice when he accepts Jesus Christ and enters into the inheritance prepared for him. God has provided everything a man needs. God is able to save every soul yielded to Him through Jesus Christ. "Wherefore he is able also to save them to the uttermost that come unto God by him, seeing he ever liveth to make intercession for them" (Hebrews 7:25). All this was known to Him when Jesus went about proclaiming the glad tidings of the kingdom of God.

OLD TESTAMENT LESSONS (6:1-4)

Jesus used more than one method in His teaching ministry. Sometimes He would draw lessons from the Old Testament, as He did when the Pharisees criticized His disciples for breaking the Sabbath when they ate some ripe grain on the Sabbath day:

> And it came to pass on the second sabbath after the first, that he went through the corn fields; and his disciples plucked the ears of corn, and did eat, rubbing them in their hands. And certain of the Pharisees said unto them, Why do ye that which is not lawful to do on the sabbath days? And Jesus answering them said, Have ye not read so much as this, what David did, when himself was an hungred, and they which were with him; How he went into the house of God, and did take and eat the shewbread, and gave also to them that were with him; which it is not lawful to eat but for the priests alone? (6:1-4).

The Pharisees were following Jesus closely, seeking to trap and to accuse Him of breaking the law. They accused His disciples of harvesting grain on the Sabbath. In answering them, the Lord went directly to the Scriptures. One reason for this would be the fact that He knew the Pharisees were expert in and had full respect for their Old Testament Scriptures. So Jesus drew attention to the story of David, who, when fleeing away from Saul, went into the house of the high priest and actually took the shewbread (put there for an understood ritual purpose), ate it and fed it to his men. Jesus pointed out that he could do this because in actual fact and need his great hunger overbalanced the ritual pattern of that time. Because the Pharisees respected the Scriptures, Jesus used this incident to show that His disciples should not have been criticized for their conduct, according to the Scriptures.

USE OF LOGIC (11:14-20)

At other times Jesus used logic or reason. He could

have told people that what He was teaching was the will of God, and that could have been sufficient authority. But He wanted people to understand, so He took time to reason with them. Luke tells of one such instance in this way:

> And he was casting out a devil, and it was dumb. And it came to pass, when the devil was gone out, the dumb spake; and the people wondered. But some of them said, He casteth out devils through Beelzebub the chief of the devils. And others, tempting him, sought of him a sign from heaven. But he, knowing their thoughts, said unto them, Every kingdom divided against itself is brought to desolation; and a house divided against a house falleth. If Satan also be divided against himself, how shall his kingdom stand? because ye say that I cast out devils through Beelzebub. And if I by Beelzebub cast out devils, by whom do your sons cast them out? therefore shall they be your judges. But if I with the finger of God cast out devils, no doubt the kingdom of God is come upon you (11:14-20).

Here Jesus is appealing to common sense. He argues that the insinuation made against Him was simply not sound reasoning and so should not be considered. The people naturally were amazed when the devils went out of the possessed man so that he was able to speak. But immediately someone was ready with an insinuation. They admitted the devils had been cast out, but said quite openly this was because Jesus was working through Beelzebub, the chief of the devils. At this point Jesus did not turn to Scripture for His comment. As a matter of fact there was probably no specific word in the Old Testament which He could have used in dealing with this particular situation. Nor did He claim any special revelation, though He could have claimed that God had revealed certain things to Him. Instead He appealed to their reason: pointing out that their insinuation was not logical. He pointed out it would be foolish for Satan to cast out the demons he had sent into the man, for he would thus only be working against his own kingdom of evil. This was a direct appeal to plain common sense.

PARABLES

The use of parables was another of His principal methods of teaching. Parables are so commonly recorded in the New Testament that it seems to be almost exclusively a New Testament word. But the word *parable* has its own meaning as *something that is highly significant.* Usually a parable is a story made up by the speaker, involving or including natural things, showing natural processes at work. When a teacher uses a parable which he is making up as he goes along, he does not mean that such an event ever actually happened.

One of the most common and well-known parables is that of the Good Samaritan. There probably never was such a definite event, although no doubt many men have been beaten and robbed, and perhaps on occasion other men have helped them. Jesus seized upon such normal happenings and used them, making stories or parables to illustrate His teaching. Simply then, a parable is a manufactured story, made up as an illustration of a certain truth which the teacher is trying to impress upon the minds of his pupils or listeners.

Just as Jesus would use logic and reason, as He would turn to the Word of God, so He would use parables. An example of this will show His method.

And he spake also a parable unto them; No man putteth a piece of a new garment upon an old; if otherwise, then both the new maketh a rent, and the piece that was taken out of the new agreeth not with the old. And no man putteth new wine into old bottles; else the new wine will burst the bottles, and be spilled, and the bottles shall perish. But new wine must be put into new bottles; and both are preserved (5:36-38).

NEW CLOTH (5:36)

In this case Jesus was using illustrations that were familiar to the people to whom He was talking. When He spoke of putting a new piece of cloth upon an old garment, He was referring to something well-understood at that time. That was, of course, many, many years before such a thing as shrink-proof fabrics were known. Cloth would be woven out of wool, in an unshrunken state, so that the first time the cloth got wet it would shrink. Thus if any woman were to take new cloth and use it in mending an old garment, she would find that as soon as the garment got wet the new cloth would shrink, tearing away from the old cloth and the hole would be larger than at the beginning. The people who heard Him teach would readily understand what He meant when He said He did not come to do a repair job. He came to provide new garments, not to patch up the old.

New Wineskins (5:37-39)

The same idea was illustrated by His reference to putting new wine in new bottles. Actually those bottles were not made of glass, but of leather, such as sheepskins. Wine put into such wineskins would ferment. The process of fermentation would result in expansion of the contents. The wineskins would expand through the stage of fermentation, stretching as the gas formed in the process. When once used the leather in the wineskin would be stretched to its limit. If new wine were put then into old wineskins that had already been stretched, and the wine began to ferment as it would, then since the skin could not stretch again it would burst. This sort of thing was well-known to the people of that day.

If the same idea were set forth in a modern illustration today, it might be something of this nature: a mechanic might say that he would not repair the motor but rather would install a new motor in the car. This would illustrate the idea that when a person becomes a Christian, the Lord does not correct habits, nor improve conduct in a man's daily living, altering the man's character a bit here and there. What He does is to give the man an entirely new life. This is what John meant when he wrote: "Ye must be born again" (John 3:7).

THE GOOD SAMARITAN (10:25-37)

Perhaps the most famous of all the parables Jesus used is the one known as "The Good Samaritan." Luke tells us that a certain lawyer had been asking questions, trying to "tempt" Jesus about His teaching. He asked our Lord what to do to inherit eternal life, and then quoted, at Jesus' request, the great commandment

> . . . Thou shalt love the Lord thy God with all thy heart, and with all thy soul, and with all thy strength, and with all thy mind; and thy neighbour as thyself (10:27).

But the lawyer was not content to stop there. He wanted to justify himself, so he asked the question, "And who is my neighbour?" Jesus answered with the famous parable so well-known:

> . . . A certain man went down from Jerusalem to Jericho, and fell among thieves, which stripped him of his raiment, and wounded him, and departed, leaving him half dead (10:30).

This parable has been called the most effective piece of literature in the world. It is claimed no other portion of literature has ever affected so much change in the conduct of people as this story of the Good Samaritan.

This parable teaches the truth about man's attitude toward man in setting forth three major attitudes toward money. First there is to be seen the attitude of the thieves. This can be expressed quite simply as "What is yours is mine, if I can get it." They took from the man, giving him nothing in exchange. Such is the disposition of a thief at all times, and as such it is utterly unacceptable in the sight of God.

Then there was the attitude of the two men who passed by on the other side: the priest and the Levite.

The beaten, robbed man had been left half dead in the
ditch by the wayside, but when these saw him they went
swiftly on their way. Their attitude was also quite clear:
"What is mine is my own, and I am going to keep it."
This is also utterly unacceptable to God.

After this the Good Samaritan came along. He looked,
saw the plight of the man and had compassion. He went
at once to the side of the man, took wine of his own to
refresh him, took oil of his own to anoint the bleeding
wounds, put him on his own beast and brought him to
an inn by the roadside. During that night he took care
of the wounded man, and when he had to leave to go on
about his affairs he left money for the care of the stranger,
giving instructions to the innkeeper to supply whatever
else was needful. He said he would settle the bill for it
on his return. This man's attitude is also obvious: "What
is mine is yours, as you may need it." It is not surprising
that the lawyer understood the point Jesus was making.

> Which now of these three, thinkest thou, was neighbour
> unto him that fell among the thieves? And he said, He
> that shewed mercy on him. Then said Jesus unto him,
> Go, and do thou likewise (10:36, 37).

In this simple fashion by the use of this parable
Jesus taught the great truth about how persons deal with
other persons in the kingdom of God. There was no reason
to mistake the meaning of this parable!

USE OF LOCAL EVENTS (13:1-5)

At other times Jesus of Nazareth taught from local
events. Luke tells of such a case:

> There were present at that season some that told him of
> the Galilaeans, whose blood Pilate had mingled with their
> sacrifices. And Jesus answering said unto them, Suppose
> ye that these Galilaeans were sinners above all the Gali-
> laeans, because they suffered such things? I tell you, Nay;
> but, except ye repent, ye shall all likewise perish. Or those

eighteen, upon whom the tower in Siloam fell, and slew them, think ye that they were sinners above all men that dwelt in Jerusalem? I tell you, Nay: but, except ye repent, ye shall all likewise perish (13:1-5).

It would appear that when these Galilaeans were going about their usual religious ritual, Pilate had put them to death, for their blood "mingled with their sacrifices." Probably they had done something to violate a Roman law and punishment was swift. This was an incident which attracted much attention in the community, and so some of the crowd told Jesus.

When He dealt with this, He made no attempt to justify God in allowing this to happen. He gave no explanation as to why these men had been killed from the standpoint of the permissive will of God. But He took that incident and brought it to bear upon the people around Him. He used their attention which was focused on what had happened to these men and taught them that such calamity, such violent destruction, is what awaits anyone who is not doing the will of God. Apparently He was not discussing the Galilaeans but used that tragedy to enforce His message to those who heard Him.

This record by Luke has its message even to this day. When calamities occur in any neighborhood, God is reminding man that life is a precious thing. Violent destruction can occur and every unsaved person, every man or woman standing alone in his or her own sin before God, should have this in mind. Any calamity is a preview of the kind of violent destruction that can and will come. Jesus of Nazareth used this incident by way of pointing to the meaning of calamity. He took the burden of guilt away from the Galilaeans as He spoke also of the men upon whom the tower of Siloam fell. He raised the question: Were the victims of Pilate's execution sinners above all in Israel? "Nay; but, except ye repent, ye shall all likewise perish."

Thus He was teaching that the meaning of calamity is not in the people who suffer death. The significance of any calamity, any disaster of any sort, is not primarily with reference to the victim. It chiefly has reference to those left alive. The victims involved are gone and cannot learn anything from the incident in question. But other people are still here. When people thus see what violent destruction looks like, they should recognize this would be the time to repent, to get in touch with God in a saving way, before it is too late.

This example will also show that Jesus of Nazareth was interested primarily in calling men to God. He was not interested especially in interpreting the affairs of the world around Him. He never offered a running commentary on the events of the day as they happened in Palestine. The gospel writers report no reference of His to these matters. Jesus apparently was committed to one thing here on earth: to call men to God. He used every circumstance, every incident that occurred round about Him to emphasize one idea in the hearts and minds of those who listened: Man must deal with God, and must turn to God in repentance, that he might have the salvation which has been provided!

THE GREAT INVITATION (14:15-24)

Jesus used a parable to teach the urgency of the necessity that man turn to God.

> Then said he unto him, A certain man made a great supper, and bade many: And sent his servant at supper time to say to them that were bidden, Come; for all things are now ready. And they all with one consent began to make excuse. The first said unto him, I have bought a piece of ground, and I must needs go and see it: I pray thee have me excused. And another said, I have bought five yoke of oxen, and I go to prove them: I pray thee have me excused. And another said, I have married a wife, and therefore I cannot come (14:16-19).

It is not difficult to see that Jesus told this parable to imply that salvation is free, and that it is graciously offered by God to all who will come in response to His call.

Jesus went on to teach in the way He told about the guests. The first guest, when notified by the servant that all was in readiness, had a fairly reasonable excuse. He had purchased a tract of land and was at such a stage in that business transaction that he could not come. The second guest had also the excuse of business, though of a slightly different nature. He had purchased five yoke of oxen, ten beasts, and the deal was doubtless pending final settlement until he had looked at the oxen and, perhaps, driven them and been thoroughly satisfied as to their quality. So this excuse was also in the natural course of a business transaction. The third guest said he was just newly wed and by this he had assumed new obligations and was bound by them at the moment. Each of these excuses have in themselves some reason for being considered adequate. But as Jesus taught the parable it would imply there is no reason on earth which is good enough to keep a man away from God. The conclusion of the parable emphasizes this:

> Then the master of the house being angry said to his serv-
> ant, Go out quickly into the streets and lanes of the city,
> and bring in hither the poor, and the maimed, and the halt,
> and the blind. And the servant said, Lord, it is done as
> thou hast commanded, and yet there is room. And the lord
> said unto the servant, Go out into the highways and hedges,
> and compel them to come in, that my house may be filled.
> For I say unto you, That none of those men which were
> bidden shall taste of my supper (14:21-24).

Thus this story of the great invitation ends on a grim note. The lesson is plain for any hearer to understand: when a person is pre-occupied with this world he actually disqualifies himself from the blessing of God. By putting this into the story of the parable Jesus in a very effective way was showing His disciples the importance of putting the things of God first. Because the parable makes use of well-known human actions the lesson is plain for every generation that reads the story: the things of God must come first!

CARE FOR THE LOST (15:1-32)

The great effectiveness of the parables as a device in teaching can well be seen in the fifteenth chapter of Luke's gospel. Here is a cluster of three parables that teach the attitude of God toward lost souls. Jesus of Nazareth had been saying such gracious things about the attitude of God toward sinners that Luke records

Then drew near unto him all the publicans and sinners for to hear him (15:1).

The Pharisees and the scribes murmured at this. They criticized Jesus for receiving sinners, and for eating with them as well. The grace of Jesus can be seen in His concern that these self-righteous objectors should not misunderstand the truth about God. He told three parables for the sake of His critics, that they might understand. These stories are commonly called *The Parable of the Lost Sheep; The Parable of the Lost Coin;* and *The Parable Seeking the Prodigal Son.* Actually they could be better named *The Good Shepherd, The Searching Woman* and *The Waiting Father.*

What Jesus was teaching these critical self-righteous people was an understanding of the personal graciousness and kindness of God when sinners turned to Him. Jesus Himself was kind to sinners. He even associated with them and no doubt made many concessions in His personal feelings to them. No one need ever doubt for a moment that Jesus Christ was always repelled by sin. He would never condone any form of sin, but He loved the sinner. In fact He was about to die for them!

This action of Jesus is something like that of a physician. The doctor will enter a house where there is smallpox, but that does not mean the doctor likes smallpox, or is in favor of it. He will treat a person with a loathsome disease because he has dedicated his life to helping the sick, no matter what their condition.

Even so with Jesus Christ, who associated with sinners because it was these He wanted to reach with His message of salvation. He told these stories by way of emphasizing to the Pharisees and scribes that God actually wanted sinners to come and find forgiveness in His grace and mercy.

THE GOOD SHEPHERD (15:1-7)

Jesus managed to convey the Gospel in the very way He told about the shepherd who went out and searched for the sheep until he found it, brought it safely home and then called in his neighbors and rejoiced. This prepares the hearer to understand the attitude of God.

> I say unto you, that likewise joy shall be in heaven over one sinner that repenteth, more than over ninety and nine just persons, which need no repentance (verse 7).

THE SEARCHING WOMAN (15:8-10)

The same was true concerning the lost coin. The point being made was that the woman searched the house diligently for the coin lost from her dowry, until she found it. She, too, called in her friends and neighbors to rejoice with her over finding something precious which she had lost. In this way Jesus is giving the Pharisees an idea that Almighty God would be glad to bring the sinners home, and when they are brought, there would be joy in the presence of the angels of God over each repenting sinner.

The Waiting Father (15:11-32)

What has been called the most perfect piece of literature in the world, the most perfect short story ever written, is what has been called the parable of The Prodigal Son. The story is actually about the father who received the prodigal son when he came home, giving him a welcome overflowing with love and tenderness. This was not because the son had been good, nor because he had done right, but because in repentance he had come to return to his father. In grace his father gave him tender mercy. When the elder brother was dissatisfied with this treatment of the younger son, the father did not chide him for his lack of love, but tried to show him that it was right to rejoice when a sinner returns with confession and repentance.

An Unjust Steward (16:1-12)

Sometimes Jesus used parables that seem strange because the principal characters in the story engaged in practices that in themselves seem unrighteous. This is a story of an unjust steward. This man had control over materials belonging to his master. Then he was called upon to give an accounting of what he had done with his master's goods. He was to have his books audited, and he suddenly realized the record would show he had not been a good manager, with the result that in all probability he would lose his job. In such a case he would need friends, and so he turned his situation to his advantage and made friends with the people who owed money to his master.

The point Jesus was emphasizing was that this world should be used in such a way as to advance eternal benefits. The steward could always live with these people whom he had befriended. Jesus was saying money here on earth should be used in such a way that it will bring benefits in heaven. When a person is through with this world and gets to heaven, there will be eternal rewards from the use made of situations in this world. No matter how many may be surprised to note Jesus' seeming approval of the actions of an unjust man, no one ever misses the lesson as to how one could use money for spiritual advantages.

THE RICH MAN AND LAZARUS (16:19-31)

In the latter part of this sixteenth chapter Luke records a famous parable, concerning the rich man and Lazarus. The story simply tells that the rich man had so much and the poor man had so little of this world's goods. When they left this world the poor man was in Abraham's bosom, but the rich man was in hell. Here again Jesus is using a parable to teach a certain truth, emphasizing mainly the importance of turning to God in this world, though He did imply other profound things in this simple story. He made it plain and clear that a man makes the decision here on earth which will bring him to heaven, or failing to make the right decision he will go to hell. This is the obvious meaning of this parable. This truth may seem harsh, but no one reading it can misunderstand it. A man makes his choice in this world. No one gets another chance. The rich man in hell begged for some relief, asking that Lazarus dip his finger in water and come and put it on his tongue. But this was impossible because of the great gulf between. Then the rich man asked that someone go back to the world and warn his brothers on earth so that they would not come where he was. This also could not be done.

This parable teaches truth of great significance for all men. The story makes it plain that the living brothers had all the warning they needed in the Scriptures: they had the law of Moses and the prophets. The message of the Bible is clear, and any willing person can know it. Actually what Jesus is giving all men to understand is that anyone can find out about heaven or hell by reading the Bible, and everyone is responsible to act upon what is written. If any man will heed the Scriptures he will be wise; if any man refuses to accept what the Bible says he is unwise and foolish and must suffer the consequences.

THE UNJUST JUDGE (18:1-8)

Jesus also used parables to teach truth that would be unwelcome to religious persons. Luke records several such parables in the eighteenth chapter of his gospel, which deal particularly with prayer. Among the Jews of His day were people who made a show of their religion by public practices of prayer. They performed ritualistic customs which included the saying of certain formal prayers, leaving the impression that when such prayers were said their part in coming to God was finished. Jesus taught in the parable of The Unjust Judge that praying should be persistent until the answer came. This is another example of His method of using an unjust person to illustrate His point. The contrast between the unjust judge who responded to the persevering widow and the righteous God who hears the prayers of obedient believers, helps to emphasize the call to persistent prayer on the part of all who do believe.

THE PHARISEE AND THE PUBLICAN (18:9-14)

In the time of His earthly ministry Jesus also found the idea common that only the good people could pray to God. The Pharisees were zealous to observe religious rules and to maintain the outward appearance of righteous conduct. In so doing they claimed they were especially qualified to be accepted of God when they came to pray. Luke records the famous parable of The Pharisee and the Publican (18:9-14) which sets forth the truth of how it is the humble and the contrite heart that qualifies a praying man for blessing. Here again in a short simple story this Master Teacher sets forth profound truth that can be instantly and fully understood anywhere, anytime among any people.

The use of parables is so obviously effective since all the world loves a story. No form of communication engages the attention so quickly as a narrative. The details of any story are easily remembered; and because they present concrete events, they are especially suitable for communicating ideas into any culture. The practical effectiveness of Jesus as a teacher is seen in that "without a parable spake he not unto them" (Matthew 13:34).

Chapter 7

THE REALITY OF DEMONS

As Luke tells the story of the public career of Jesus of Nazareth he reports remarkable occasions in which Jesus showed control over natural processes and events. The miracles He worked have been considered in their significance showing that He was indeed the Son of God in the flesh. Not only did these works of wonder manifest the power of God which He could use whenever He wanted to, but the very nature of what He did in healing, in restoring, in restraining gave clear indication of the benevolent purpose of God in blessing man through the work of Jesus. As Nicodemus said, "No man can do these miracles that thou doest, except God be with Him" (John 3:2).

The truth is that Jesus of Nazareth saw men in their pathetic need, in their weakness, their sickness and their sin. He demonstrated His purpose to redeem, to deliver and to restore man in the grace of God, whenever any would turn to Him. He did this by showing the power and authority only God could exercise, to the amazement of all who saw Him.

LUKE'S APPROACH

Luke's account of the works of Jesus of Nazareth was written without explanation. Because He was a physician, Luke could be expected to offer some reason, or at least to point out some conditions which would always accompany any miracle. But he does not do this. He is content to present a simple record of the events as these occurred.

110

This characteristic of Luke's ⟨...⟩ ⟨re⟩markable and shows something important about ⟨...⟩ God. Luke tells of the healing of the leper, bu⟨t⟩ ⟨...⟩ no discussion of leprosy as a disease nor any con⟨...⟩ ⟨...⟩n of any means Jesus may have employed to effect ⟨hea⟩ling. He tells of the healing of the dumb man, bu⟨t th⟩ere is no examination of the condition of being unable to speak. Luke reports that Zacharias did not speak, but there is no clear description to show that he could not, nor is there any reference to any psychological block which rendered him speechless. Luke points out that the woman with the issue of blood was incurable, but there is no description of the flow of blood to show its nature nor to explain why the woman could not be helped by any physician. He tells the amazing story of the palsied man in simple terms but offers no explanation of what happened. He reports that Jesus stilled the storm on the sea by His personal uttered command, but there is no discussion of the physical elements involved to show how this was done. He tells of the feeding of the 5,000 with a few loaves and fishes, and while he does note the baskets filled with leftover food, which shows this miracle really happened, there is not one word of explanation that would give any clue as to any procedure. This silence as to means employed or procedures followed is actually an impressive testimony to the effect that the works done by Jesus of Nazareth were supernatural. They have the character of being spiritual in their origin and in their performance (John 3:8).

Luke never leaves any doubt as to the reality of the situation in which Jesus did His work. The leprosy was real. The dumb man actually could not utter words. The issue of blood was treated by physicians at the cost of "all her living." The storm at sea actually threatened to sink the boat. The 5000 were fed with actual food of which 12 baskets of fragments were taken up. It is true the procedure of Jesus in solving these problems was never analyzed; the events were not described in specific detail;

but there could never be any reasonable doubt that the works of Jesus were real exhibitions of power and authority.

The record given by Luke gives no basis for the idea that anyone is to learn how to do similar works by recognizing and using the principles and the processes involved. Luke gives no instruction, offers no guidance, presents no challenge which would call for the willingness or the abilities of any person to try to do likewise. Each work of Jesus is reported as a direct exercise of the power of God to the glory of the living God. Rather, the story told by Luke seems to aim at encouraging souls to trust in the living God who alone can work, does work and will work through the Son of God to achieve the purpose of the Father.

Truths Seen in the Miracles

In all such miracles several truths are to be seen which are important for any understanding of the work of salvation. First, God is the Saviour: Man does not achieve salvation by his own efforts – it is the gift of God who is active in the whole event. Second, salvation is not the result of natural processes: the power of God controlling the natural by His will saves the man out of his distress. Finally, salvation is by the grace of God through faith: it is not necessary, nor is it possible, for man to earn this blessing by anything in himself – it is the free gift of God.

> For God so loved the world, that he gave his only begotten Son, that whosoever believeth in him should not perish, but have everlasting life (John 3:16).

It is important to recognize that no man can do what needs to be done in his own strength. Every human being has in himself only that which is natural and this is inadequate for living in the will of God (Matthew 16:17; Romans 8:8; I Corinthians 2:14; 15:50). Also man himself is sinful and cannot do even what he wants to do (Romans

7:14-25). There is hope for man only because God will help him through grace (James 4:6; Romans 5:20,21).

All things done in the natural way are spoken of as the work of nature, and all that is done by the power of God according to His promises, is called grace. God made nature. He is the God of nature. There is nothing happening in the natural world but what God causes to happen. Sun, moon and stars obey His will. But the natural man is not obedient to God because of sin. Man's inward disposition is warped. Inside every man is a twisted nature. The grain of the wood in any man's soul is crooked. Put man under pressure and break him open: the crookedness will show. Man is not straight and can never straighten himself out, but God is able and God is willing to do this for man by His grace through His Son.

REDEMPTION OUT OF NATURE

God has always had a plan for the redemption of man out of his sinful nature. Jesus Christ is "the Lamb slain from the foundation of the world" (Revelation 13:8). It is true that man is born into the world of nature without his consent. It is also true that God sent His Son into the world to redeem without being invited. But the Gospel is presented to the consciousness of man and he is called to accept the grace of God in Jesus Christ which is able to save him. Jesus of Nazareth came into this world to show men what God could do and would do for them by His grace. He called men to trust God and to allow Him to save them through His power in His grace.

The fact that nature cannot help man out of his sin can be felt by looking at the natural world. Poets may glorify nature and artists may paint its beauty, but in nature there is no mercy to be found. Nature does not pity nor protect the bird with the broken wing: the cat gets it. The wolf easily catches the rabbit with the broken leg; nature does not pity it. The beautiful lake, which the artist was so eager to paint, will drown the innocent baby and never shed a tear. In nature men die. Amid all the beauty and grandeur of tropical forests, islands and mountains, benighted heathen live in sickness and fear. Only the Gospel of the Grace of God can bring hope of salvation.

All this seems to be implied in the account given by Luke of the works of Jesus of Nazareth. The work of Jesus is always gracious, adequate and free: it shows the benevolent love of God. But there is no hint that such works are possible in the course of natural processes, by any result of natural factors, forces or intelligence. What Jesus manifested was none other than the wonderful works of God which are done in the natural world by the power of God who made this world and can control it by His will.

There is a type of God's grace which is manifested in kindness to mankind, a common grace in which all His creatures share. The sun shines, rain falls, food is available; but the kindness of God as shown in nature does not go beyond death. Yet in the grace of God as manifested in Jesus Christ "everlasting life" is promised. God went far beyond all natural processes in grace by bearing the sins of man in His own body. He takes away man's guilt by suffering in his place, delivering any man from the load of sin once and for all, if that man will accept His atonement through His Son.

The Lord Jesus came to bring salvation because man is in trouble. Man is not strong enough, clean enough, and cannot have an acceptable record. His intentions are usually bad, so that good purposes are not often his goal. Man is not good enough to face the issues of daily living, so man is in distress and difficulty. There is not a human being who knows his right hand from his left who does not feel guilt. Men fail to live up to their own standards, let alone God's standards. There not a person with any sense of discrimination at all who fails to realize that within himself he is unclean. Furthermore (and this can be even worse) men are in bondage in daily living. Many times men do foolish things, even when they don't intend to. This happens over and over again.

In His public ministry, when Jesus of Nazareth began to preach and teach, He showed to men and women that God is able to set a man free from this bondage. First He showed that God can deliver man from natural troubles. He came to men who had physical limitations and helped them. He opened the eyes of the blind. This was a temporal condition, but God could restore the function of the eyes He had created, and He did so. Some had ears which had stopped functioning, and He unstopped them so they could hear again. He loosed tongues so that men could speak. He restored a withered arm. He made the lame to walk and raised the dead. All such works were in the realm of the physical.

MIRACLES BENEFIT THE PERSON

In all that Jesus did, there was real benefit to the person in question. These works were not fantastic in any sense of the word. For the sake of illustration, Jesus did not make a blind man see with his ears or his hands. He restored vision to the eyes which were made originally for seeing. When a man could not hear, Jesus did not touch him so that he could hear through the tips of his fingers. Ears were made for hearing. Nor did He attach another set of ears; He healed the ones that were "in trouble," as it were. He took the paralyzed, atrophied parts of the body and made them come alive again. For the sake of emphasis let it be noted that when the Lord touched the man sick of the palsy, helpless on his bed, He did not make that man fly like a bird; He simply restored him so that he could walk normally. In the works He did, Jesus restored man to God's original intent and purpose. This is a marvelous suggestion as to what He came to do for men. He restores man to what God wanted man to be.

The saving works of Jesus of Nazareth went beyond that which was physical. Luke tells of a number of occasions in which Jesus cast out demons. This may well be an area in which little is known to men, but the gospel story is quite simple and plain. There can be no question that Luke says plainly that Jesus of Nazareth dealt with demons.

Students of human nature today recognize and study conditions which they feel produce symptoms similar to those referred to in the gospel narratives. In their analysis of such conditions scholars often fail to give credence to the reality of demons. It is natural today to reach the conclusion that in the days of Jesus there really were no demons. But this is not acceptable to anyone who takes the gospel of Luke to be true.

Who Are Demons?

The words *devil* and *demon* are used interchangeably in the Authorized (or King James) Version of the Bible. The text will speak of a *man possessed of the devil,* or of a woman *out of whom went seven devils.* In other passages the word *demon* is used; devils and demons are one and the same thing. The real question is: are they real?

It will help to remember that Luke did not think of demons as being little *pixies,* little brown men who sit on coat collars and whisper evil suggestions in men's ears; nor *elves* or *gremlins.* These various ideas have caught popular imagination at one time or another. But the truth to be understood in the gospel story is more. Demons are spirits. They do not have physical bodies. Men could not see them, nor hear them, nor sense their presence. However the story told by Luke makes it clear that they are real, they do exist. The narrative reports what happened in such a way that it seems they are persons.

A well-educated man, a learned professor of psychology once asked a student of his, who was a Christian, how it was possible to think of God as a person. The professor admitted this was a real difficulty to him, even though he might want to become a Christian. The student asked him, "What is the idea of person in the mind of a psychologist?" The professor replied "You know enough psychology to know that we have no clear idea what a person is." The student then pointed out, "If you as a psychologist cannot say what is meant when anyone calls me a person, is it not natural that you certainly could not understand what is meant when I speak of God as a person?" This simply demonstrates that modern culture does not have the ideas, the terms, the language with which to grasp what is meant by a "person" in the spiritual world.

The student asked the professor, "Do you think I am a person?" The professor cordially replied, "Yes, I do." The student went on to say "Good. And I think you are a person. And I think God is a person."

There was a time when no one could say anything about electricity, because they didn't know about it. But electricity was real and working in those days. Paul would say that in those days it was a "mystery" which afterward became known. Even so with the nature of God: because psychologists do not have the language to think of Him as a person does not change the reality of God at all.

Despite the inability of men trained in social sciences to grasp the idea of person, people generally use this term and are normally understood when they talk. It may be helpful to note that there is an old classic definition of person that actually fits common sense use today: "A person is a being who can think, feel and will." Because God knows He can *think;* because God has compassion He can *feel;* and because God controls and directs He can *will.* Thus it is proper to say that God is a *person.*

All that has been said of God would of course apply

to the Holy Spirit, who knows the needs of Christians and so can *think;* He can be grieved, so He can *feel;* and He can send out missionaries, so He can *will.* This emphasizes the fact that a being can be a person who does not have a physical body.

When once it is recognized that to be a person does not require a physical body, it is easier to think of God as a person, and the Holy Spirit as a person. A certain young couple lived in a community where they were thought of as neighbors. At a bend in the highway their white house could be seen. That house was the spot where they lived. One night their house was burned to the ground. The next day no one could see the white house. The house was gone, but the young couple were still neighbors. In time they built a new house where they now live.

Not long ago my son-in-law died suddenly. On my way to the funeral I went by the funeral parlor to look at the body. My granddaughter riding along in the car told me "You won't see my daddy in there. That is just the house he lived in." The body, the earthly house, was in the casket; but the spirit, the person, was gone. Paul would say in comforting believers that Christians will have heavenly "houses" prepared for them to live in eternally.

Just as God and the Holy Spirit are to be known as persons though they are Spirit and do not have physical bodies in which to dwell, so angels, Satan, and demons are to be known. The Bible does not say much about angels by way of identification. No description of angels is given. The word angel means messenger and, like the words doctor, farmer, or carpenter, refers to what they do, not to what they look like. Some are named: Michael the Archangel and Gabriel. But that they exist and that they act in service to God is a matter of record (Matthew 18:10; Hebrews 2:7-16, etc.).

In the light of this discussion demons are to be classed as persons. Throughout this whole consideration it will be helpful to keep in mind that what is true of God as a person, and the Holy Spirit as a person, is to be taken as true of Satan as a person. No human being has ever seen either the Holy Spirit or Satan in any natural way. The Bible tells about both, and what the Bible says makes it clear that as one is a person so the other is a person. In the same way, as angels are living beings with characteristics as persons, so demons are living beings with characteristics as persons.

WHAT IS DEMON POSSESSION?

What is meant when it is said that a person is *being possessed by demons?* It means that the victim is literally under the will of another: some other entity is in control of the man's will. Psychologically, this would be like being *filled with the Spirit.* A person who is filled with the Holy Spirit is a person whose consciousness is dominated by God in Christ Jesus. Just so a person who is possessed by a demon is one whose consciousness is dominated by Satan through one of his evil angels.

The phenomenon of one person dominating or exercising control over another is not uncommon in human affairs. Much of what happens in consciousness may have a bearing on a person's physical condition. Much progress has been made during recent years in the area of psychosomatic medicine. Today the average medical practitioner would recognize that a person's mental condition may affect his physical condition. The opposite is just as true; the physical condition may affect the mind, although perhaps not to the same extent. People can be in a state of mind which will affect them: either to making them ill or to aiding them physically. In the light of such facts, the question arises as to whether or not an evil being, influencing the mind, causing imbalance, could so disturb the consciousness and arouse the emotions to affect seriously the operation of the personality. This would actually hinder the physical processes of the body, and make the victim susceptible to sicknesses of one kind or another. Such would seem to be the implication of certain statements in the gospels (Luke 13:16).

There is another aspect of this whole matter that could be briefly examined to advantage. No doubt everyone has heard of the phenomenon of hypnotism. In this case the mind of one person is yielded to the mind of another person. Perhaps the word *mind* is not precisely correct at this point, but it can serve to refer to the mental and spiritual aspects of the personality. A person's consciousness, including his will, can be yielded, as far as his spontaneous initiative is concerned, to the control of a second person, so that he can be put under an hypnotic spell. This does not happen without the consent of the subject, but a person can agree to be hypnotized. In the state of hypnosis the person may not know what he is doing. Generally, when the hypnotist gets his subject under his control, he tells the subject what to do. It has been most interesting to note that by such suggestion by the hypnotist the subject can be prompted to do things which he would normally not do. The full significance of this phenomenon has not yet been recognized in personal conduct. The principles of hypnotism may be operating in subtle ways that escape recognition, but are nonetheless important.

I recall a demonstration put on in an advanced class in psychology. The professor announced to his class that he would demonstrate what he called *post hypnotic influence*. He explained that he would put some willing student under hypnotism. While in this condition he would tell the subject what he would do after he came out of the trance. These would be foolish things which that student would not normally do. All of this was explained to the class while the subject was out of the room, so that he knew nothing about it. He only knew he was to be part of an experiment, but for what purpose he did not know.

The demonstration was begun, and after the subject

was hypnotized he was told what he would do after he came back to normal. Said the professor: "You will go back to your desk and sit down. I will be lecturing and I will set up a certain illustration by way of experiment. I will ask for volunteers to go to the blackboard and put thereon answers to questions I shall ask. You will be one of those volunteers. I will ask every volunteer to put his name at the top of his work, so we can identify each one. You will put down the name of *Smith*. I know Smith is not your name, but it is the name you will put down. We will all see it and we will laugh at you, but you will do it nonetheless. When I ask you why you did it, you will laugh it off and say you don't know why, you just felt like it.

"After you have completed your exercise at the blackboard and returned to your seat, you will think that the room has grown very cool. It will seem to you the wind is blowing in strongly. You will get so cold that you will go and close the window near to your desk."

This demonstration was put on during a hot summer day, and the wind was not blowing. Students were reminded to note that the subject would be entirely out of the hypnotized state when he would go quietly to shut that window! The professor made clear in his initial briefing of the class that though the instructions would be given while the subject was under hypnotism, he would be brought out of the trance and would *then* follow the instructions without realizing he had been so instructed.

The experiment proceeded as outlined. The student was brought out of the trance. Later the professor stopped his lecture and asked for five or six volunteers to come to the blackboard. This student came, along with the rest. "Now," said the professor, "in order that we may identify your work, write your name at the top of the blackboard where you will work." Everybody did as told, and this student wrote *Smith*. Everyone laughed. He did not know why they laughed, but thought it was because he had written *Smith*. The professor said, "Why did you write *Smith?* That is not your name." The student replied, "Oh, just for the fun of it." Everyone in the class was shocked and appalled, but they concealed their feelings. So the student went on with the exercise and returned to his seat. The professor went on lecturing. In due time the student pulled his coat together around him, rubbed his arms, and gave evidence of feeling cold. Finally he yielded to this, got up quietly and went and closed the window near his desk. A quiet hot day! Ridiculous? Unreasonable! Yes, but horribly true! That man did what he did because the idea was implanted in his mind by another person, while he was under the hypnotic spell.

Much more attention could be given to the whole phenomenon of hypnotism to learn about spiritual influences. It is common understanding that the hypnotic spell is induced by focusing all attention and interest on some one thing: a bright light, a shrill noise, etc. This seems to imply that if anyone has some one proclivity or appetite, he might be tempted to focus attention and desire in such a way as to concentrate on it to the exclusion of other ideas, and Satan could use that state of mind for his own purpose. He can make that particular idea or object so attractive that a person will be tempted to lose sight of all else, until he desires it so completely that he will lose all self-control. During that time of being entranced, it is possible suggestions will come to him, as if they were "in his bones," as it were. He wakes up in the morning, is called to breakfast, and must go about his day's work. He looks normal, and goes about his duties as if he were normal, yet a day or two later, or some time later, he will do the very thing that came into his mind days before when his thoughts were so concentrated upon that desired satisfaction. If these ideas are sinful or hurtful the thoughts did not come from God. Perhaps it could rightly be said that such a man was truly under the influence of an evil spirit. Such may well have been the case of Mary Magdalene, out of whom seven devils were cast.

How Christ Controls

When a man is a Christian the most wonderful idea he ever had is that Jesus Christ died for his sins. In the sight of that everything else can fade out. Jesus Christ dying on Calvary's cross for him enthralls any soul. When a man feels afraid of God (when he is ashamed of himself), and does not have the courage to turn to God, he can look at Christ Jesus on Calvary's cross and his heart will melt. Thus he will take fresh hope, as he worships God in the Person of Jesus Christ. This is the real purpose of church worship. This is the need in church services, to focus attention upon Jesus, who loves the sinner, who gave Himself for sinners and set believers up to be a kingdom of priests unto God.

There is a good sense in which the believer, while in that state of being, is practically lifted out of himself, being enthralled as he concentrates on the Person of Jesus Christ. Something happens to this man which is like being hypnotized: the Holy Spirit coming into the inner being, prompting the person, makes definite suggestions as to desirable future conduct.

One can always expect certain results after such an experience. There may be times when the believer reminds himself that he wants to read a portion from the Bible, even though he usually doesn't understand the portion he does read. He may feel he should pray, and so he kneels down to pray, although he may have many things to do, and actually be very weary. The believer will pray, even though perhaps he does not feel much result. The man may think he ought to talk to someone about Christ, or to invite a certain person to come to church, or to visit a certain member of his church who is in the hospital. Such practical conduct could appear as a consequence of the soul being under the influence of the Spirit of God. With the contact set up in the worship service the Holy Spirit may move the man to some task for God. What a wonderful thing it is to be filled with the Spirit! Then one can leave the results to Him after following His leading. The Bible seems to promise this to be possible for any believer.

While the Son of God was here in the flesh He exercised His will and set men free. He is able to control evil; He can control Satan. He can say to any evil spirit, "Come out of him," and the devil will come out. He is Lord of all, and He has complete victory over Satan and all his hordes. That is the safety of the believer. Is there danger, is there peril because of evil spirits? Yes, all men are in danger and peril! Men are always in danger of death while they live, but Jesus has won the victory over death!

THE CHRISTIAN'S WITNESS

In Acts 26, when Paul was presenting his great defense before Agrippa, he told the king why he had been sent to preach the Gospel of Christ:

> To open their eyes, and to turn them from darkness to light, and from the power of Satan unto God, that they may receive forgiveness of sins, and inheritance among them which are sanctified by faith that is in me (Acts 26:18).

Here then was the commission of Paul, the apostle: "to turn them from darkness to light, and from the power of Satan unto God." By whom are the souls of men to be influenced? To whom are believers committed? Whom does the believer take to his heart? Are men to be deceived by some personal wish or whim, through some private yearning? through some inward desire? Are souls to be taken captive by the deceitfulness of sin so that they covet certain things, thus being actually led away from God? Or will Christians look into the presence of their Lord and Saviour, Jesus Christ, with such a plea from the hearts:

> Search me, O God, and know my heart: try me, and know my thoughts: And see if there be any wicked way in me, and lead me in the way everlasting (Psalm 139:23, 24).

Believers need to throw themselves upon His mercy, trusting Him to keep them, that they may say with Paul:

> . . . for I know whom I have believed, and am persuaded that he is able to keep that which I have committed unto him against that day (II Timothy 1:12).

Something of this truth can be felt when one listens to Paul, speaking again to Timothy and advising him as to his conduct concerning certain men who had gone the wrong way:

> And the servant of the Lord must not strive; but be gentle unto all men, apt to teach, patient. In meekness instructing those that oppose themselves; if God peradventure will give them repentance to the acknowledging of the truth; And that they may recover themselves out of the snare of the devil, who are taken captive by him at his will (II Timothy 2:24-26).

The influence of Satan was a very real thing to Paul, and he made this clear in his instructions to the Corinthians at one point:

> For to this end also did I write, that I might know the proof of you, whether ye be obedient in all things. To whom ye forgive any thing, I forgive also: for if I forgave any thing, to whom I forgave it, for your sakes forgave I it in the person of Christ; Lest Satan should get an advantage of us: for we are not ignorant of his devices (II Corinthians 2:9-11).

It would be a helpful practice for each Christian reading this to ask himself soberly, *"Am I ignorant of the devices of Satan?"*

Paul wrote that significant word above at a time when Christians were having trouble with one of their own number. He urged that believers forgive one another graciously so that the chance for alienation will be lessened. Christians should never let hate develop, for this is where Satan comes in. Paul said, "To whom ye forgive any thing, I forgive also." One of Satan's devices is to divide and separate Christians. Wise Christians will be careful. This truth can also be heard from Peter:

> Be sober, be vigilant; because your adversary the devil, as a roaring lion, walketh about, seeking whom he may devour: Whom resist stedfast in the faith, knowing that the same afflictions are accomplished in your brethren that are in the world (I Peter 5:8, 9).

In view of this peril is there any reason as to why Christians should be in despair? The answer to this lies in the area of commitment. Every believer should ask himself plainly and often: "To whom am I committed?" "No man can serve two masters," but any Christian can be sure of one thing. If he puts his hand in the hand of the Lord Jesus Christ, he will never need to fear Satan. The only time any believer needs to be afraid is when he turns his back on God, when he departs from the living God. Why would anyone do that? Why do children ever get lost? When a mother is walking through a department store, why does her little boy suddenly get lost? Is it not because he saw a toy or some other interesting object which claimed his attention so that he turned aside to look at it? Then, his eyes perhaps caught a glimpse of something else in the next aisle and his willing feet took him further and further away until he was lost. His mother had called him, but he didn't come when he heard her voice. Something else attracted him more, and so he was *willingly lost.* In the Book of Hebrews it is written:

> Take heed, brethren, lest there be in any of you an evil heart of unbelief, in departing from the living God (Hebrews 3:12).

No, you won't ever need to be afraid, if your daily walk is close beside the Lord Jesus Christ, for Satan cannot trap those who live close to the Lord, whose hearts are in His care and keeping.

No man can serve two masters: if a man has Christ Jesus as his Master, then Satan never will gain that power over him. The devil goes about "as a roaring lion seeking whom he may devour," but the Christian need not fear, if the Lord Jesus Christ is his defense. The basis for confidence is expressed in a well-known couplet, which is absolutely gloriously true:

> Satan trembles when he sees
> The weakest saint upon his knees.

There seems to be no valid reason to doubt that demons are alive and active today under the control of their master, Satan. One of the common difficulties of Christians today is that when the Bible is read as the Word of God, this whole teaching about demons is overlooked as if it were not there. The result is that many persons in their naive ignorance are being brought under bondage. Christians generally do not have sufficient intelligence either to understand what is happening, or to know how to go about defeating it. All that is needed is to come to Jesus Christ. A person does not need to understand Satan and all his ways. It is important to recognize his power and to fear it, and to believe at the same time that Jesus Christ is in control.

Let me add a purely personal note to say how thankful I am to God that it has never been my disposition to take any pleasure in jokes or amusing stories about the devil. I am thankful I have never wanted to tell such a joke and I have never heard one that I felt was funny, or that I wanted to laugh at. This situation is far too serious. Do you know why I feel that way, as to the seriousness of Satan's power as a created being? Jude 9 reports:

> Yet Michael the archangel, when contending with the devil he disputed about the body of Moses, durst not bring against him a railing accusation, but said, the Lord rebuke thee.

Beloved, Satan is a powerful being, and it is disturbing to hear Christians talk so lightly and so flippantly about him. He is not a light person, nor is he anything like the cartoons one can sometimes see. It is wholesome to avoid having anything to do with him. The life of every believer is in the hands of the Saviour, and no Christian needs fear Satan. But a person would be very ignorant spiritually if he did not realize that Satan coveted his soul.

Luther had his experiences with Satan. Many things have been said and written about the tremendous faith and understanding of Martin Luther. According to his own testimony Luther actually had dealings with Satan. The devil was so real to Luther that at one time he picked up a bottle of ink and threw it at Satan! Some will say, There must have been something wrong with Luther. There was! He was a sinner and he knew there was a struggle going on as Satan contended for his soul. Luther was in a sinful world, face to face with the great issues of the reality of sin. His personal testimony is very significant. In his great hymn, *A Mighty Fortress is our God*, Luther wrote that as far as Satan was concerned, "one little word shall fell him."

This leads the mind back to the temptation of Jesus in the wilderness. "One little word" as referred to by Luther would be the word of Scripture, and the Lord Jesus resisted Satan in the desert by quoting the Word of God to him. Any Christian who will read the Bible to get its truth into his heart and soul and mind will have a protection far beyond anything that can be described.

There are many other aspects about the truth of demons particularly along the line of their relationship to health. There is no doubt that one's mental condition has a direct bearing upon one's physical welfare. When the mind is energized, activated, inspired by an evil, malevolent, malicious being such as demons are, the result can be along the lines of actual sickness and physical bondage.

When a Christian reads his Bible and comes to passages dealing with demons or devils, it is not wise for him to slip over such Scripture and dismiss it from the mind as just an old-fashioned way of referring to sickness of mind or personality. It is just about as old-fashioned as talking about God, heaven, the angels, the Holy Spirit. Actually, these beings exist today just as they did when Jesus walked the earth. But one can always remember that He has gained the victory over Satan, and this can give peace. The Scriptures report that at the word of Jesus Christ, Satan as the leader of demons and all his hosts, must obey. All a Christian needs to do is to stay close to the Lord Jesus Christ. He is our adequate, complete protection against all these evil forces. Apart from our Lord the picture would be a dark one for any man. With Him, indwelt by the Holy Spirit, victory belongs to any-one – "whosoever believeth in Him."

Chapter 8

THE GENERAL TEACHING OF
JESUS OF NAZARETH

In the very way He went about His ministry, Jesus
of Nazareth was a teacher. He did not come to show
man what He could do, nor how He could do it. As
Luke tells of the works and the teachings of Jesus he
makes it clear that Jesus made no attempt to open up
natural processes to show the inherent possibilities in
nature. Natural processes could never do His works. Nature in itself, including human nature, can be vitiated,
blemished, warped; it is sinful.

In nature if anything goes wrong, death follows. This
is true also of the spiritual nature of man. "The soul
that sinneth, it shall die" (Ezekiel 18:20). This truth is
clearly seen in the plant world. A plant which does not
adjust properly to its surroundings withers and dies. Even
grass, which flourishes for a time, finally withers and
dies. This is the rule for all nature, including natural
human beings. There is no living thing in all nature which
has not the sentence of death implicit in it. Living in
the natural world means, actually, keeping one step ahead
of death. Nothing taught by Jesus of Nazareth denied
this natural fact of death.

As a natural person, man can be very conscious of
the reality of death. If the heart should stop beating there
is no way to keep life in the body, and man cannot make
his heart beat! Thus man has the sentence of death in
himself. When a person becomes ill some part of the body
is not functioning properly, some part of the natural organ-
ism is not living up to its full potential, and so sickness

results. If the sickness is not cured, death takes over. Where does infection come from? Where does the pus come from which gathers in a wound? Where does the congestion come from that fills the lungs? Must something come into the body? No, the potential for infection is already in the body.

If anything happens so that the refuse of the body cannot be eliminated: such as if the pores of the skin cannot breathe, or a clot of blood forms to stop circulation, then infection will speedily set in. The person becomes ill, and eventually death results unless this condition is remedied. Death is with the natural man moment by moment, day by day, even as he breathes. When a man breathes in, he takes in fresh air; when he breathes out, the air from his lungs is no longer fresh: it is now carrying out some of the waste material cast off by the body. If the body breathes in impure, tainted air, the whole system will be poisoned by it. All of this is in the realm of nature, and all men are more or less aware of this truth.

THE NEW CREATION

The Son of God came into this world to show to conscious, living human beings another way of living. He told men that God would *save:* but this process of saving does not mean that God will stop the process of death in the natural body. It means that God will regenerate, not into another natural state as a sort of second chance; but into a different spiritual state. A person who is *born again* is a "new creature in Christ Jesus." Natural life comes by generation from father and mother. The body is born of the mother. Spiritual life, however, does not come from earthly parentage.

Spiritual life comes directly from God as the person receives His promise and believes Him. Something happens inwardly that goes far beyond conviction. Conviction is essential to salvation, but it is involved only in the beginning. When a person believes in the Lord Jesus Christ and receives Him as Saviour, committing himself to Him, something happens in the heart. This is called *being born again:* becoming "a new creature" or creation in Christ Jesus. The believer is now an entirely new person. However, it is still true that such a redeemed soul can learn from the past experience and past mistakes of the old life, as far as the things of this world are concerned.

This new creature, the spiritual nature now living in the believer, has several distinctive characteristics. For one thing, *it cannot die.* One reason for this is, that which is born of Christ Jesus does not sin. The old man sins, and the old man (the human nature) will die. Eventually the physical body will be buried six feet underground and the old nature will pass away. That will be a glorious day when the believer is finished with it. The environment of this world will pass away, but the soul and spirit will not pass away. They go directly to the God who gave them. This is the truth reported in the Bible, which the Son of God came into this world to show to mankind. This is the different way of living in this sinful old world of ours.

The life in Christ Jesus is not merely a better way of living so that the believer will be better off than he was before. It is true that culture can show better ways of living. Civilization also can show better ways. There are many avenues of approach by which attempts can be made to improve human nature. It is like soil in a garden. If it is allowed to lie there, without any cultivating, there will not be much growing in it. But when it is cultivated, with fertilizer added to enrich it, this soil can be improved, to the point of raising a good crop of vegetables or beautiful flowers.

Normally any garden will produce according to the work that is put into it. The same principle is true in bringing up children. There is no doubt that training a child is all very good; in fact along certain lines it is absolutely necessary. When a well-educated person comes to face life on his own, he is more competent in whatever field he enters; he is more capable, better able to get along in the world and probably will be more prosperous. But one thing will always be true. No training, schooling or culture can possibly achieve what Jesus Christ came to do in human hearts and lives. In his letter to the Galatians, Paul said, about this very truth:

> . . . for if righteousness come by the law, then Christ is dead in vain (2:21).

The Son of God did not come to show how the law could work in guiding men to blessing. He came to show how grace could triumph: how by the grace of God sinners could be transformed, regenerated into something entirely different. No one can ever fully exhaust the riches of this glorious truth of what God will do for believers in Christ Jesus. It should be always remembered that Almighty God is willing, ready and able to save to the uttermost all who will come to Him through Christ Jesus. Salvation brings peace, joy, assurance . . . , with every blessing man could want. Quietness of mind and heart will come as a gift from God, when the soul puts his trust in the Lord.

WHAT LUKE RECORDED AND OMITTED

All this can be seen clearly in Luke's gospel. He makes it plain that Jesus of Nazareth in His public ministry, did not try to show what *man* could do, but to point out what *God* would do for anyone who would deliberately commit himself to God according to the promises He has made. God will bless man in His grace and mercy as a free gift, the only condition being that man turn to Him. This is the wonderful truth of the Gospel. Jesus Christ came to give His life a ransom for many, because the Father sent Him. He taught them, showed them the Father by His deeds in their midst, died for them, rose again and even now is sending His Holy Spirit to guide and comfort them. It is very clear in all that Jesus did that salvation is the work of God.

In this discussion miracles have been looked at as a sample of God's almighty power. Parables have been noted as our Lord's way of teaching and of showing God's truth. The works of power which He performed have been sent as demonstrations of God's power in delivering the human spirit from the bondage of evil forces, evil spirits, which are referred to as devils or demons. It has been recognized that these demons are as real as the Holy Spirit is real, and that Satan is as real a person as Jesus Christ. In the reading of Luke's gospel it becomes clear that all such facts are not a matter of personal preference or desire, but a simple report of things as they actually are. There is much that is beyond human understanding. Yet the point seems simple and clear: it is a good thing to trust God. He knows what He is doing. Jesus of Nazareth had complete confidence in His heavenly Father.

Luke offers no explanation as to why God created man so that there is a possibility of his being lost, nor why Satan is permitted to exercise the power he has in this world. Whatever may be the truth about this in the permissive will of God, there is no reason to feel that God was compelled so to do. Jesus of Nazareth never undertook to explain this, but He did reveal truth that is most reassuring. He made it clear that God calls men to trust Him, and that He is able to save man in any given situation. No matter how malevolent Satan may be, nor how dangerous, he cannot harm anyone who trusts in the Lord God Almighty.

UNDERSTANDING FAITH (5:1-10)

Trusting in the Lord must be understood to be an active thing. A person doesn't trust in Him because he has signed a piece of paper, such as a decision card. *Trust* means that at any and all times the soul may call upon Him and be confident of His immediate response and His power to deliver. To communicate these ideas Jesus of Nazareth at times used certain actual circumstances as a setting for teaching truth. An illustration of this is to be found in chapter five of Luke's gospel:

> And it came to pass, that, as the people pressed upon him to hear the word of God, he stood by the lake of Gennesaret, And saw two ships standing by the lake: but the fishermen were gone out of them, and were washing their nets. And he entered into one of the ships, which was Simon's, and prayed him that he would thrust out a little from the land. And he sat down, and taught the people out of the ship (5:1-3).

This particular incident happened at the lake shore where there were two small fishing boats, probably some sort of rowboats. Apparently there was a large company of people on the shore. In order to be seen and heard more easily Jesus asked to have the one boat move out a little bit, probably having the anchor rope loosened so that the boat was allowed to drift away from the shore a short distance. Luke does not report what He talked about to this large group of people. It is probable that the "Sermon on the Mount" in the gospel of Matthew (chapters 5-7) and the "Sermon on the Plain" in Luke (chapter 6:20-49) will show the general trend of His message. He would be giving the sort of message John the Baptist had preached. No doubt He talked about understanding the law of God, the reality of God and the reality of man's relationship with God. No doubt it was His custom when Jesus reached a certain point in His message, that He would demonstrate His meaning. This may have been His purpose when He said to Simon,

> Launch out into the deep, and let down your nets for a draught. And Simon answering said unto him, Master, we have toiled all the night, and have taken nothing: nevertheless at thy word I will let down the net (Luke 5:4, 5).

There is much to learn from noting how this incident developed. Jesus of Nazareth is to be seen here as a teacher, a rabbi; Peter is a veteran fisherman. When Jesus directed Peter to go out to catch fish, Peter told Him that the fishermen had just come in from a night of experience that proved there were no fish running. It would be known that Peter and his co-laborers were fishermen by trade; they would know the best places and the best times to fish. It was clearly Peter's opinion that this was not the time. It would seem that Peter greatly respected Jesus of Nazareth for he went on to say, "Nevertheless at thy word I will let down the net."

In this action Peter set an example of acting in obedience even when there was no natural evidence to support that choice. This would still be a valid response even today. Doubtless many more would receive the blessing of the Lord if men would obey what is written in His Word, even if it does not seem practical.

It is not unusual to find that a Christian, though burdened, might say, "There is no use in praying about *that*, no use at all. I have prayed about it for months. I know all the circumstances, and prayer will accomplish nothing." Such a person should ask himself whether the Word of God would direct him to continue in praying, not because he had confidence that things would work out, but because the Scriptures call him to pray. The Christian might be surprised as Peter was surprised here. When Peter and his co-workers did let down the net they "enclosed a great multitude of fishes: and their net brake" (verse 6). Apparently God can and will do more than even His believers can ask or think.

As Luke records this incident he seems to point out one supreme truth: believers must obey God to find out how great He is! The greatness of God is never seen unless men act. If God's Word is heard and is obeyed even with misgivings and doubt, any man can learn of God's power and greatness. When God commands, He enables and fulfills His promise. God always honors His Word. There is no other way to find out how truly great God is.

This truth can likewise be recognized in the matter of praying. Suppose a believer has on his heart a burden about some other person. Suppose the Christian gives much thought to the situation so that he feels he can explain all the difficulties involved and can understand the whole matter clearly. Suppose the Christian sees it all from a human point of view. In that case it may seem there is no way out, no hope for the victim in trouble. Now suppose the Christian becomes aware of some promise in Scripture which he feels is relevant. The Bible encourages him to ask in faith that he might receive the blessing.

> Ask, and it shall be given you; seek, and ye shall find; knock, and it shall be opened unto you: For every one that asketh receiveth; and he that seeketh findeth; and to him that knocketh it shall be opened (Matthew 7:7,8).

A definite answer to this prayer would not only be an astonishing result for the skeptical believer, but it would greatly magnify the name of the Lord in the hearts of all who knew of the whole matter. It seems quite clear that if a man will not ask he will never receive; and if he never receives he cannot ever know how great God is. If a believer doesn't seek, he won't find; and if he doesn't find, he will never know how great God is. And if a believer doesn't knock, the door won't be opened: and if the door remains closed, that man will never know how great God is!

This whole spiritual experience can be started by God revealing some aspect of His great plan to us. In such a revelation God gives some kind of call to take a step by faith. The person so-called may look up to tell God the proposed action is foolish. It is possible such a person may not realize how bold and how dishonoring to God such unbelieving arrogance actually is. Such disobedient response actually reveals a self-satisfied confidence in one's own judgment. It is a case of assuming that the person's own knowledge equals or exceeds the knowledge of God. But if that person will admit that God can do more than he can ask or think, that person, despite his skepticism may act, and just as surely as he obeys in line with God's revealed Word, he will find out how great God is! By obeying the command he will learn more than he expected to learn.

This wonderful truth can be learned even in a negative way. Suppose that the person called by the Lord to act in line with God's revealed Word is so full of misgiving and doubt that he does *not* obey the call of God. This person will of course have no results and so for him there is no learning about God. In this case unbelief will become more and more dominant and this person will have less and less appreciation of the greatness of God.

The Centurion's Faith (7:1-10)

Luke records another illustration of the general teaching of Jesus Christ in chapter seven:

> Now when he had ended all his sayings in the audience of the people, he entered into Capernaum. And a certain centurion's servant, who was dear unto him, was sick, and ready to die. And when he heard of Jesus, he sent unto him the elders of the Jews, beseeching him that he would come and heal his servant. And when they came to Jesus, they besought him instantly, saying, That he was worthy for whom he should do this: For he loveth our nation, and he has built us a synagogue. Then Jesus went with them. And when he was now not far from the house, the centurion sent friends to him, saying unto him, Lord, trouble not thyself: for I am not worthy that thou shouldst enter under my roof: Wherefore neither thought I myself worthy to come unto thee: but say in a word, and my servant shall be healed. For I also am a man set under authority, having under me soldiers, and I say unto one, Go, and he goeth; and to another, Come, and he cometh; and to my servant, Do this, and he doeth it. When Jesus heard these things, he marvelled at him, and turned him about, and said unto the people that followed him, I say unto you, I have not found so great faith, no, not in Israel. And they that were sent, returning to the house, found the servant whole that had been sick (7:1-10).

The centurion (a term for an officer in the army) was in all probability a Roman officer who had favored the Jews, having made a contribution to help them build a synagogue. This was a truly unusual thing in that day. Because he had helped the Jews, so that they considered him as a friend, he had no hesitancy in asking the Jews to convey his message to Jesus. He had heard of this prominent teacher who was reported as having unusual powers, and the best approach to reach Him seemed to be through his Jewish friends. So they came to Jesus and brought this request, saying of the centurion that he was a good man, who "loveth our nation, and he hath built us a synagogue."

As Jesus drew near to the home of the centurion, the Roman sent his friends out to say, "Don't come any nearer, Lord, for I am not worthy. You do not have to enter my house, and thus earn the social criticism which would fall upon you." This man had asked for Jesus' help, and this would seem a somewhat strange way of welcoming the one who was to help him. But the Jews and the Gentiles had very little dealings with each other at this time in this place. There was no social contact of any kind, and Jesus was after all a Jew in His earthly body. Only under unusual circumstances would a Jew enter a Gentile home and Jesus risked severe criticism in doing so now.

But the centurion added even more protest. He said, "I didn't feel worthy enough to come in person and talk to you. I didn't think I was a fit person to come into your presence, but I have faith to believe you can heal my servant without even coming into my house. I, too, have authority, and my servants do as they are told. You can exercise your great authority without having to enter my house." Jesus marveled. He commented that not in all of Israel had He seen such remarkable faith. What kind of faith? Faith that Jesus had authority over the elements causing the sickness, and that His word was powerful.

Jesus took the centurion at his word and did not go any nearer to his home. But when the servants returned to report to their master, lo, the chief servant was well again, fully restored to health and strength. One sentence in this account, reported as spoken by the centurion, shows the whole meaning of this incident:

. . . but say in a word, and my servant shall be healed (verse 7).

This is the kind of faith that the Son of God honored. There is an important lesson in this incident. Confidence in the power of the Lord to do what is asked is vital to a living faith in Him. When a promise is read in the Word of God, or is heard from some witness, does the heart have confidence that He can perform that promise? God looks on the heart of any praying person. He is pleased to see faith that believes He is able. The centurion believed, and Jesus marveled in appreciation of that faith. When the heart responds in full confidence that God can, this is an important factor in the consequence that God will hear and answer the prayer.

A FORGIVEN SINNER'S LOVE (7:36-50)

In the latter part of chapter seven there is another incident reported that serves well to illustrate the method of teaching employed by Jesus of Nazareth.

And one of the Pharisees desired him that he would eat with him. And he went into the Pharisee's house, and sat down to meat (verse 36).

The Pharisees were a highly-regarded class of people. That Jesus of Nazareth would have personal fellowship with a Pharisee shows that He would seek to help all classes of people, including those who were highly esteemed in the community.

Pharisees held the Scriptures to be the Word of God. They had only the Old Testament but they believed not one jot nor one tittle of the law would pass away until all was fulfilled. A Pharisee considered Scripture to be the literal Word of God, and undertook to obey every requirement to the letter to win the blessing of God. Nicodemus was a Pharisee and was a good man. Saul was a Pharisee and served God with a clear conscience even in his ignorance and unbelief.

In this incident one of these very religious men, a Pharisee, invited Jesus to a meal in his house. Jesus did not confine His acceptance of invitations to one class or another. Here He was eating with an "up-and-outer," a man who was a leader of the people religiously. It is true that Jesus elsewhere was accused of sitting at meat with a sinner, a tax-gatherer. It is a wonderful thing that the Gospel is for the "up-and-outers" and the "down-and-outers" alike. God makes no distinction in the sin or the sinner; all are alike in His sight. There can be people who live virtuous lives, who are kind to those in need, and who are exemplary members of the community, and yet do not know God. It is to be remembered that Jesus died for them, too, and they should be told of this.

While they were sitting at meat something unusual happened:

> And, behold, a woman in the city, which was a sinner, when she knew that Jesus sat at meat in the Pharisee's house, brought an alabaster box of ointment, And stood at his feet behind him weeping, and began to wash his feet with tears, and did wipe them with the hairs of her head, and kissed his feet, and anointed them with the ointment. Now when the Pharisee which had bidden him saw it, he spake within himself saying, This man, if he were a prophet, would have known who and what manner of woman this is that toucheth him: for she is a sinner (7:37-39).

The description of the woman is clear: she was known to be a sinner. The context brings out the fact that she was publicly regarded as a sinner, a woman of the street, notoriously of bad reputation and character. This woman

coming into the house where Jesus was eating was not
violating any social custom. In that society houses were
more or less in the open, as a modern patio or summer
house would be. It was not the social custom that one
must stop at the door, to be admitted and announced.
People could come in and go out at will. Such customs
still prevail in some places today. Missionaries tell that
natives come and go, in and out, as they see fit. And
so this woman came in.

In coming into the house of the Pharisee with an
alabaster box of ointment to anoint the feet of Jesus, this
woman was not doing anything at all extraordinary. In
the custom of the time washing and anointing the feet
of a guest would be as if someone came to visit on a
hot and humid day, and a servant would bring the visitor
a cooling glass of iced tea.

It is quite possible that this woman really had no
intention of washing His feet with her tears. She probably came to *anoint* the feet of Jesus with the ointment
she brought. Such anointing might seem strange today.
Apparently it would be something like using lotion or
hand cream for soothing purposes. In those days people
walked everywhere practically barefoot, with open sandals
on their feet. It was the common custom upon entering
a house to take off the sandals, and walk in barefoot.
If the host intended to give a gracious welcome, a servant
would bring a basin of water and rinse the dust of the
road from the feet of the guest. The servant would then
dry the feet of the guest on a towel. It seems apparent
this woman came in the fashion of a servant, to show
Jesus normal courtesy.

Such a ceremony of welcome could end with the
drying of the feet, but an unusually careful and gracious
host might add the anointing with a perfumed ointment.
So this woman took a box of perfumed ointment which
she had brought with her. It was very costly, for she
brought the best she could obtain.

No doubt as the woman took the ointment to anoint

His feet something was happening in her heart. Her tears began to gush forth, born of the reverence, the joy, the affection she had, as her heart truly overflowed. Since she was not a servant, she had brought no towel. Doubtless the washing of the feet had not been in her mind. But as her tears splashed on His feet, she wiped them dry with her hair. With His feet so close to her face as she dried them with her long, flowing hair, it was a simple matter to place a kiss of reverence on those feet. Then she anointed His feet with the precious ointment. It is probable that in this whole incident nothing very unusual as to procedure was noticeable.

But while this little ceremony was in progress, the Pharisee, Simon by name, became very critical. He did not understand how Jesus could tolerate the touch of this woman, and so condemned Him in his heart. "If this man were all He claims to be," thought Simon, "He would know what kind of a woman this is, and He would instantly turn her away. He would know her for a woman of the street." Such thoughts in the mind of the Pharisee were probably not so unusual or strange. For quite naturally He would think that Jesus, if He were a prophet of God, with the sensitivity of a man who is spiritually minded, would recognize a sinner when He saw one, and that He would react by drawing away.

What happened then was no doubt a great surprise to the Pharisee. Evidently Jesus knew the woman, and He also knew what Simon was thinking. At once He turned to him:

. . . Simon, I have somewhat to say unto thee. And he saith, Master, say on. There was a certain creditor which had two debtors: the one owed five hundred pence, and the other fifty. And when they had nothing to pay, he frankly forgave them both. Tell me therefore, which of them will love him most? Simon answered and said, I suppose that he, to whom he forgave most. And he said unto him, Thou hast rightly judged. And he turned to the woman, and said unto Simon, Seest thou this woman? I entered into thine house, thou gavest me no water for my feet: but she hath washed my feet with tears, and wiped

them with the hairs of her head. Thou gavest me no kiss:
but this woman since the time I came in hath not ceased
to kiss my feet. My head with oil thou didst not anoint:
but this woman hath anointed my feet with ointment.
Wherefore I say unto thee, Her sins, which are many, are
forgiven; for she loved much: but to whom little is forgiven, the same loveth little. And he said unto her, Thy
sins are forgiven . . . Thy faith hath saved thee: go in
peace (7:40-50).

The story speaks for itself, but there is one point that
could well be brought out. It would be easy to think that
Jesus said, "Her sins, which are many, are forgiven,"
because the woman had washed His feet and anointed
them. But there seems no doubt that if she had not been
a forgiven woman, she would never have come near Him.
If she had not realized that her sins were forgiven, she
probably never would have touched the feet of Jesus.
It seems quite likely that here is a woman Jesus had met
before, a woman with whom He had dealt, a woman
whom He had delivered from her bondage, whose sins
had truly been forgiven. When she heard He was in the
house of Simon, she came with the most precious thing
she owned, to anoint His feet. She wanted to do something for Him. He understood that, and He so interpreted
it to Simon. In the conversation Jesus pointed out to
Simon that he had not been forgiven much, but this woman
had. Her sins had been many, so that she had been forgiven much. It was for this reason the woman loved him
so much.

No one need ever feel sorry because he has not been
forgiven much. All that is necessary is to take a candid
look at self. If any man has difficulty seeing how much
he has been forgiven, he need only think of what he should
have been with the insight he has. Perhaps he knows
about prayer. Then he should have been praying, and
this he has not done. He may know much about the good-
ness of God. In that case he should have been thankful.
Perhaps he needs to learn humility of heart. The degree
of a person's feeling of sin is variable. It depends upon

how the individual personally feels. In the latter part of his life, as an old apostle, Paul said to Timothy,

> This is a faithful saying, and worthy of all acceptation, that Christ Jesus came into the world to save sinners; of whom I am chief (I Timothy 1:15).

Paul had the great gift of true humility. When he says he was the chief of all sinners, this does not mean he was the greatest chicken thief in the country, or that he went around stealing the belongings of other people, or killing other men. No, that is Paul's own estimate of himself. When he came to see the Lord Jesus, the more he saw of Him, the more profound was his realization of his own sinfulness, and the deeper his gratitude for his forgiveness.

Recently there was reprinted a book called *The Memoirs of Murray McCheyne*, a famous Scots preacher. He was a wonderful man, a preacher of unusual gifts, reared in a Presbyterian manse in Scotland. He had never lived a wicked life nor caroused around as a youth in a life of dissipation. He died at the age of thirty three, and it was said of him that he was the holiest divine Scotland ever saw. It is reported in his Memoirs that he was often crushed to the ground with a sense of his awful sins. He had no crude, outward, vulgar social sins, but he sensed the distance between his barren soul and Almighty God, so great in His holiness. Though he lived a good life, as men would say, he felt himself to be a great sinner. This is is a wonderful spiritual truth. The more a man can see the depth of his sins the more he can see the wonderful grace of God. And the more one sees of His grace, the more profound will be one's gratitude and love for Him, for "We love him, because he first loved us" (John 4:19).

Luke sets out the account of what has been called, The Transfiguration of Christ, in 9:28-36. There is one important fact in that most significant passage: Jesus of Nazareth was always God. On the Mount of Transfiguration He was not changed! He was simply revealed. When

His face became shining as the midday sun and His garments were glistering white, when Peter, John and James looked on Him and were overwhelmed with a sense of His glory, it was not because He was different. It was only that His glory was being manifested. It had, up to that moment, been covered up. Every day Jesus lived in this world He *was* the Son of God, but on that Mount of Transfiguration what had been inside was brought into the light of day for a brief moment for Peter, James and John to see.

THE DISCIPLES' PROBLEM WITH DOUBT (19:37-43)

When they came down from the mountain they found that certain of the disciples could not cure a boy who was afflicted. This was a serious matter. While Jesus and the three disciples were up on the mountain, the nine other disciples were down among the people teaching and ministering to the crowd. A distressed father had brought his afflicted son to the disciples of Jesus for help. The disciples tried to cast out the demon possessing the lad, but could not do so. Their failure was a shock and an astonishment to the people.

No doubt there are many families who are not coming to church, even though they believe the church is the house of God. They will not listen to the preacher, although they believe he is a man of God. They do not think about nor spend time with the Bible; yet they believe it to be the Word of God. It is possible for such people, no matter what their private world of suffering or trouble, to think to themselves that some day they will come to God, some time they will turn to Him. And they expect something to happen when they do come.

Every now and again one of such people may come to church. Whenever this happens, it is not a matter of ordinary routine. Such men and women feel strange when they walk into a church. They may not have been inside the house of God for a long time. Even now they have not come because it is a Presbyterian, or a Methodist, or a Baptist church; but because they believe, down deep in their hearts, that it is the house of God. They came because they want to draw near to God. They may need some special help from Him.

Perhaps some mother has worked and worked, prayed privately and long to get her wayward son under the sound of the Gospel, and finally she prevails upon him to accompany her to church. Oh, what a tremendous responsibility for the preacher whoever he may be. The preacher may not be aware of the wayward son in front of him. Will he then be speaking the Word of God on that day when that man comes? Will he be preaching the Gospel in power that day when the needy soul sits before him? How often it happens that some teen-ager is finally prevailed upon to come to church – and nothing really happens at all! Oh, the despair and deep doubt which can then be generated in the hearts of concerned persons, when the preacher has failed to preach the clear Word and to present the real challenge of the Gospel of God's grace!

This is the only man on record who ever came to Jesus of Nazareth expressing doubt as he came. He is the only man who ever said to Jesus, " . . . but if thou canst do any thing; have compassion on us, and help us" (Mark 9:22). The leper did not come that way, but said, "Lord, if thou wilt, thou canst make me clean" (Matthew 8:2). Martha did not come that way. She said, " . . . Lord, if thou hadst been here, my brother had not died. But I know, that even now, whatsoever thou wilt ask of God, God will give it thee" (John 11:21, 22). The Bible reports that persons came to Jesus with confidence, except this man who had brought his son to the disciples and found they could do nothing for him.

Is it not possible that one of the reasons for widespread, deep unbelief in our communities today is the weak, inept, ineffectual, impotent activity going on around the church? People can come, bringing their children, and then have to take them home again no different than when they came. Adults come to the church service, listen, take part in the worship service as best they know how, go out after a handshake from the preacher, being no different than when they came into the house of God. Oh, may the Lord forgive and give insight and understanding to His people. Christians need to pray for each other.

When this incident occurred the disciples were deeply concerned. The moment Jesus had delivered this lad, and he and his grateful father had left, the disciples came to Jesus asking Him privately, "Why could not we cast him out?" Jesus told them plainly, "Because of your unbelief." Then He said unto them, "This kind can come forth by nothing, but by prayer and fasting" (Mark 9:28, 29). In other words, their spiritual strength was not great enough. Their attitude was one of unbelief. It is soberly true that a man can believe in Jesus Christ and yet lack faith to believe the Lord can accomplish what is desperately needed in his life. Oh, the grace and patience of our wonderful Lord who waits for His own believers to come to Him in their need!

ZACCHAEUS (19:1-10)

There is yet one more incident to note, and it is about Zacchaeus. He is well-known as the little man who climbed up in the tree. At this point an important truth is to be seen. When Zacchaeus climbed up into that sycamore tree, he was not a believer in the Son of God. He was simply a curious person who wanted to see Jesus.

> . . . he sought to see Jesus who he was; and could not for the press, because he was little of stature. And he ran before, and climbed up into a sycamore tree to see him, for he was to pass that way (19:3, 4).

But now something happened, an amazing thing, a startling thing. As Jesus walked by, He turned and called to Zacchaeus to come down! How glorious is this truth! Any day any person looks to see the Lord, he is due for a wonderful surprise. The Lord is looking for him. When a man looks, even if he doesn't know what to believe, he will find that the Lord has His gracious eye on him and is calling him to come to Himself. Jesus called Zacchaeus to come down, telling him that He wanted to eat a meal in his home. And Zacchaeus came down, as fast as he could, and ran "and received him joyfully" (Luke 19:6).

There is no report as to how long Jesus remained in that home, but the testimony of Zacchaeus was very positive when He was ready to leave: "Behold, Lord, the half of my goods I give to the poor; and if I have taken any thing from any man by false accusation, I restore him fourfold" (Luke 19:8). This would indicate the man was converted, changed from what he had been before. What changed him? Fellowship with the Lord Jesus Christ. How did he obtain this fellowship? He just looked to see Him, and lo, the Son of God was looking to see Zacchaeus. He called him to Himself, so that then and there Zacchaeus' curiosity became a living faith!

Chapter 9

BETRAYAL, TRIAL AND CRUCIFIXION

Luke tells the story of the last twenty-four hours in the earthly career of the Son of God in chapters twenty-two and twenty-three. It is obvious from the report that the death of Jesus of Nazareth was no accident. It was no interruption of His plans. There is no need to look at the death of Jesus Christ as if it were a calamity that He was cut off that way. This is what He came to do, and in it He accomplished the will of His Father.

The one thing that needed to be done was that men should be forgiven. The burden of his sin would have hindered any man from coming to God, just as the barrier of his sin, which would have prevented God from dealing with him, needed to be taken away. In ways that are far more wonderful than men can even begin to understand, God had planned it from the very beginning: the way to get rid of sin was to take it on Himself. He would pay the penalty. He did this in His own Son, the second person of the Godhead, according to a plan that was in existence before the foundation of the world. The plan was that God would save for all eternity such creatures of His as would commit themselves to Him, in and through the Lord Jesus Christ. So, when Jesus of Nazareth came into this world, He was born to die in payment of God's penalty for the sins of men.

Paul says it something like this: Though Jesus was equal with God, He did not think it a thing to be grasped or to hold onto to remain equal with God, but emptied Himself, made Himself of no reputation, and being found in fashion as a man, He humbled Himself and became obedient unto death, even the death of the cross (Philippians 2:6-8).

Then why had Jesus come? He came to die for sinners. To be sure He did many works, but such were done by way of identifying Himself before the people. Anyone who could work those miracles must be God. And so, after a ministry of approximately three years, fulfilling the Old Testament prophecies so that people would remember that He had done exactly what the Old Testament said the Messiah would do, then He could say, "The hour is come. The Son of man is to be glorified." From that time He deliberately moved toward the cross.

It is important to recognize this purpose in the career of Jesus of Nazareth. It is so natural for people who want to be right in the sight of God in their own conduct to think that Jesus tried to show men how to live. No doubt in a secondary sense that's true. But in the primary sense He came to die in order that men might live. That was the real aim of His career.

As far as teaching men is concerned, the first thing Jesus taught was how to die, because only as man learns how to die will he know how to live. As a matter of fact, in Christian experience a man must die in the flesh that he may live in the spirit; he must be buried with Christ in baptism that he might be raised with Him in newness of life. Thus, in understanding Christian experience, it is necessary to recognize the resurrection life, the new life. It is obvious there can't be a resurrection without previous death. The only way a man can be resurrected is to have been dead. And if any soul is going to live in resurrection life he must pass through this experience of being crucified with Christ.

When Jesus of Nazareth moved to His crucifixion He was reaching over, as it were, to put His hand on the door knob that He might open the door of heaven for believers in Him. That's the route the believer will go.

The way of the cross leads home. And there *is* no other
way, no matter what kind of signposts men may put up
(John 14:6).

Public Opinion Favored Jesus (22:1-2)

Luke begins his report of the incidents of the betrayal,
trial and crucifixion of the Lord Jesus with a significant
comment about public opinion at that time.

> Now the feast of unleavened bread drew nigh, which is
> called the Passover. And the chief priests and scribes sought
> how they might kill him; for they feared the people (22:1,2).

When Luke writes that they "sought how they might
kill him; for they feared the people," he is reporting that
they couldn't kill Him openly. If those in opposition to
Jesus hadn't feared the people they could have killed
Him openly and been done with it. But the people thought
Jesus was a good man. They had been so often blessed
by His kindness and His mercy that they would have re-
sented and rebelled against any ill treatment given to
Him. Mob action would have resulted against the chief
priests and scribes. And so they were forced to scheme
His death in some cunning way to escape the wrath of
the common people. They might never have been able
to figure out what to do if it had not been for the action
of Judas Iscariot.

The Role of Judas (22:3-6)

> Then entered Satan into Judas surnamed Iscariot, being of
> the number of the twelve. And he went his way, and com-
> muned with the chief priests and captains, how he might
> betray him unto them. And they were glad, and covenanted
> to give him money. And he promised, and sought oppor-
> tunity to betray him unto them in the absence of the multi-
> tude (22:3-6).

In chapter seven of this present study consideration
was given to demons, demon possession and being under
the influence of demons. That's what is to be seen here.

Satan had not always been in control of Judas. His ideas had not always been in the heart of Judas. No one should think about Judas as being a lying, scheming, conniving man from the beginning. He probably did not join the apostolic company in order to get something out of them. This was a ministry into which he was called. He was called as eleven other men were. This made him one of twelve selected persons. Evidently he enjoyed the confidence of his brethren. He was treasurer, and it is not hard to see he must have been a man of good report if he was going to be treasurer of a group of twelve Jews. There is no reason to doubt that such an one would be a person in whom they had full confidence.

It seems important to realize that Judas could have been a good man. No man would be in the apostolic company who would not have been rated as a good man. It is true that John says he was a thief – and apparently John means that was his character. Does that necessarily mean that Judas was a burglar or that he had a criminal record, or even that he had ever stolen anything? Before a conclusion is reached, one should raise the question: when is a person a thief? When he steals? In that case what was he before he stole? An honest man? If so, how could he steal? Honest men don't steal. If Judas had been an honest man, John would not say he was a thief. Actually, a man has to be a thief to steal. If he didn't steal before, it was just that he didn't have a chance to do it. There are any number of thieves around today not stealing anything, because the police force is too good. They'd steal if they got the chance. When John says that Judas was a thief he was doubtless referring to his inordinate love of money.

In any case, by way of noting a bit further that Judas was probably not a notorious character, it may be recalled that when Jesus a little later says that one of His disciples, one of the Twelve, is going to betray Him, no one suspected Judas. They began to inquire which one of them it would be. No one thought it would be Judas.

Actually, John reports that each one said, "Lord, is it I?" This is a wonderful tribute to their humility, but it also is evidence that Judas was not notorious. Apparently Judas enjoyed their respect and their confidence. There seems no reason to doubt that he was a good man by human standards. But Satan knew that Judas had a weakness: a secret, private, covetous feeling which made him a victim of Satan when the time came. Apparently he was not always under the sway of Satan. But this night he fell under Satan's control, because of his love of money.

No doubt the question has been asked often as to how Judas could betray his Master for any price. It is possible to hold a dime so close to the eye that one can't see the sun. A dime may be small, but it can shut out the light of the sun. Satan held out thirty pieces of silver, and those thirty pieces of silver looked so big to Judas that he lost sight of Jesus. Without fully realizing what he was doing he chose the money. In what followed this act there is more proof of the kind of man Judas was. When he realized what he had done, he went back and threw the money on the floor of the temple. He said he wouldn't have anything to do with it, that it was dirty money. They told him that that was his own problem. They had paid him and that was that. He went out and hanged himself. This may seem to be a futile procedure, but it is further evidence that Judas had a good man's conscience. An inherently evil man wouldn't have had that kind of remorse.

Every natural thing about Judas seems to have been against what he did in betraying Christ, except one thing: his love of money. That's a sobering thought for anyone. A perfectly proper prayer, for a Christian to pray at all times, is found in Psalm 139:23: "Search me, O God, and know my heart: try me, and know my thoughts: And see if there be any wicked way in me." Each believer needs to recognize his own weaknesses and confess them to God, that He might deal with them.

The Last Supper (22:7-27)

Luke tells about the last supper when Jesus arranged to eat the Passover with His disciples, and includes in his account what is called the institution of the Lord's supper.

> . . . he took bread, and gave thanks, and brake it, and gave unto them, saying, This is my body which is given for you: this do in remembrance of me. Likewise also the cup after supper, saying, This cup is the new testament in my blood, which is shed for you (22:19,20).

So on that last occasion when He was together with them, Jesus solemnized not only the occasion, but showed them how it was to be actually a form, a ritual to follow, a sacrament to keep, which would remind them that He died for them. At this point one could ask what did Jesus want His disciples to remember? He doesn't say: "Remember how I dealt with that poor man; remember how I treated that sinful woman; remember how I helped this person over here who was in trouble." That's not what He mentioned. He told them to remember the one supremely important thing that He did when He offered His body to be broken, His blood to be shed for many for the remission of sins.

The very origin of Christian experience is the conscious rejoicing in gratitude because Christ Jesus gave Himself for sinners. This is what He wanted His followers to keep in mind. It would be easy to forget. It would be natural to begin to think that the reason God is blessing the believer is because he is good. For this reason it is important now and again to break the bread and remember this is why God can be good to men: Christ died for sinners, to take the cup and realize that this is why God deals in mercy with men: His blood was shed for them.

"But, behold, the hand of him that betrayeth me is with me on the table" (22:21). It would be hard to pick one passage and make it seem more important than any other, but in some respects this one may deserve special attention. Perhaps, of all the poignant grief the Lord Jesus endured here upon earth, there was nothing so peculiarly hard for Him to bear as that someone who lived with Him for three years and had been entrusted by Him, would sell Him out for thirty pieces of silver. It is sobering to read in the Book of Zechariah about Messiah the Prince, standing in the presence of God, and when the people see Him, some will say, "What are these wounds in thine hands? Then shall he answer, Those with which I was wounded in the house of my friends" (Zechariah 13:6).

"And truly the Son of man goeth, as it was determined" (Luke 22:22). Judas might suddenly get the idea of doing it for thirty pieces of silver, but God knew he was going to do it all the time. If God hadn't permitted this, it never could have happened. Judas might still have wanted money, but it is likely he never would have had the opportunity of going through with this.

"The Son of man goeth, as it was determined: but woe unto that man by whom he is betrayed!" Sometimes people wonder whether Judas was responsible for what he did. Yes, he was responsible. No amount of argument to any other end has any bearing on this point. Each person stands before God according to the purpose and the intent of his heart and mind. That is how men are judged. Of course God is able to make even the wrath of man to praise Him, and it belongs to the glory of God that the things which men do in sin God can reverse and turn around to produce blessing. But that's no credit to man, nor is it any excuse for his conduct.

"And they began to enquire among themselves, which of them it was that should do this thing" (verse 23). That's the way Luke reports it, but John reported it more directly. According to John they began to ask the Lord, "Is it I?" These were not proud men. Notice how humble they were. When they heard that one in the crowd was to be a betrayer, notice that they didn't say, "Oh, oh, I doubted him all the time." They didn't have in mind some other person. They were not critical of each other. Each felt he might be the weakling. They were humble in spirit. Each felt he personally was probably the most unworthy member of the group.

Immediately following this report of their personal humility is the record of their interest in personal prestige. Luke writes, "And there was also a strife among them, which of them should be accounted the greatest" (22:24). In His answer Jesus laid down the principles which should guide His followers forever. He pointed out that it is the fashion of the world to exalt their rulers and to ascribe all manner of excellence to them, as well as to give them the highest honors. He then went on to say:

> But ye shall not be so: but he that is greatest among you, let him be as the younger; and he that is chief, as he that doth serve. For whether is greater, he that sitteth at meat, or he that serveth? is not he that sitteth at meat? but I am among you as he that serveth (22:26, 27).

It would never be misunderstood as to who He was. The Lord Jesus was no servant. He was Lord, King of kings and Lord of all. He was the Son of God. All the hosts of heaven worship Him and leap to do His bidding, but He took the lowly place of a servant while He was here on earth. Think of this. If anyone wants to be great in spiritual things, let him be ready to do something for someone in the name of the Lord. Then be ready to do something more for someone else, and then again for someone else. Let him be willing to do something more and more until nighttime. Then let him get up the next morning and continue to do for others. Such a person will *be* great! The nice thing about it is that there is so little competition when it comes to service. There are so many opportunities. Everyone is willing to let the other person do it. A wise person will just go ahead and do it. And all the time he is doing for others, the humble soul is drawing nearer and nearer to Him who came to give Himself in service.

Peter's Testing (22:54-62)

The story of Peter as one of the apostles is well-known to Bible readers. No doubt he was unique as a person, yet many of his experiences are typical for all believers so that much can be learned by studying the events in which he was involved. In Luke 22:31-34 we have the account of how Jesus of Nazareth warned Peter of a spiritual testing he would have to endure.

> . . . the Lord said, Simon, Simon, behold, Satan hath desired to have you, that he may sift you as wheat: But I have prayed for thee, that thy faith fail not: and when thou art converted, strengthen thy brethren.

The language implies that Satan could not get Peter until he had permission. Satan cannot do with any soul as he pleases. He would like to get control of a person and shake that one to show the weakness in him, but he cannot touch anyone except as God permits him. Satan asked for Peter. Something similar happened in the Book of Job. Satan asked God to have the privilege of testing Job, and he was allowed to do so. Satan tested him all right, but Job remained true to God in his patience. Likewise Peter was to be tested as the account later reports. It happened very soon after this warning. Jesus knew this would happen and spoke to Peter to prepare him to endure the testing.

The Bible reports that Satan is under control. He cannot do with men as he pleases, but believers may fall into his hands as Peter did. Yet the Lord does not forsake His own. Jesus saw beforehand that Peter would fall into this testing, and He prayed for Peter that when he got into this trouble his faith would endure and bring him through. And then, with that experience of having been so upheld in the hour of trial, Peter was to strengthen his brethren. In this way the wiles of Satan would be escaped.

The actual event of the testing occurred when Peter was confronted in the presence of the soldiers and the other people milling around there. Some individuals confronted him with the fact that he was one of the apostolic company and belonged to Jesus of Nazareth. This was what Peter vehemently denied. It was this denying experience, this being tested in such fashion, that was like taking wheat and putting it on a sieve, then shaking it and sifting it so that the chaff would blow away. Satan's idea concerning Peter was this: "You let me shake him real well; I'll show you there's nothing to him but chaff." It was to the glory of Jesus that Peter eventually withstood this temptation to desert His Lord.

This whole incident shows an amazing truth. A believer can have more faith than he has good sense. A believer can have more faith than he has steadfastness. Peter faltered, but he never doubted. This is important to note. A Christian may feel about himself that he hasn't done what he should have done. This may be true, but he should cling to what he has – his faith in the Lord. That's how it was with Peter. He fell in the temptation. He denied His Lord, yet he still believed. This is what brought him through.

The wonderful truth seems to be that the Lord Jesus reached hours ahead into Peter's life and prepared him for his time of testing. That night Jesus told him, and it happened early the next morning. It was as if Jesus reached forward and held Peter up by His own grace. That's what He meant when He told Peter, "I have prayed for thee, that thy faith fail not." It should be noted He didn't say: "I prayed for you so that you wouldn't be tempted. I prayed for you in such a way that you would not have any trouble." What He did say was: "I prayed for you so when trouble comes and you are tempted, if you should fail, you won't let go of me; I prayed that your faith would endure. Then when you are clear of this whole matter you can strengthen your fellow believers."

This whole incident is all the more impressive when it is remembered how confident Peter had been in his own faithfulness. When Jesus had announced all would forsake Him, Peter "said unto him, Lord I am ready to go with thee, both into prison, and to death. I'm ready to die." There need be no doubt about his meaning well, despite the fact that just a few hours afterward he denied he ever knew Jesus. There was probably no question in Peter's mind as to what he intended. It must have been a shock to him when Jesus said, "I tell thee, Peter, the cock shall not crow this day [the rooster won't crow in the morning], before that thou shalt thrice deny thou knowest me" (22:34). It would seem that believers can be much weaker in themselves than they realize.

It seems evident that Peter meant what he said about being willing to die for the Lord Jesus. "When they which were about him saw what would follow [that they were going to arrest the Lord Jesus], they said unto him, Lord, shall we smite with the sword? And one of them smote the servant of the high priest, and cut off his right ear" (22:49, 50). From other gospel accounts it is clear this was Peter. If a man taking his sword and tackling the whole Roman army means anything, this is what he was ready to do. And yet, this man who was ready to die in the heat of battle, was the very man who fell when there wasn't any battle. Because someone was making fun of him Peter tried to hide. He was the same man. This shows human nature: men are so undependable, men are so fickle in their testimony. There wasn't anything wrong with Peter's intention. Actually it was confidence in his own strength that was the fault in this matter.

GETHSEMANE (22:39-46)

As Luke goes on with his story he tells about Gethsemane. This offers a study on prayer which will repay much attention. It is important to note that Jesus Himself went into Gethsemane. He who was the Son of God was confronted with this terrible issue that was before Him: that to accept the will of God meant being separated from His Father in death.

> . . . he was withdrawn from them about a stone's cast, and kneeled down, and prayed, Saying, Father, if thou be willing, remove this cup from me: nevertheless not my will, but thine, be done. And there appeared an angel unto him from heaven, strengthening him. And being in an agony he prayed more earnestly: and his sweat was as it were great drops of blood falling down to the ground (22:41-44).

Here is an instance of spiritual tension that human beings can scarcely know anything about. There seems no reason to think He was afraid to die physically. Many lesser men have been willing to die. There was much more involved than mere physical death. It seems that One who had never done a thing wrong was to be made sin. Sin was that which Jesus hated, which he loathed; and He was to be made sin. Also this event meant He was to be separated from His Father, whereas from eternity He had been with His Father! It is difficult for any human mind to think of this. There were aspects of this event in Gethsemane that no human being can ever grasp. How the mind of Jesus responded to His Father men may never know, but something was done there that left Jesus in complete peace as He went out to face the coming tragic events.

Luke tells very simply that He allowed Himself to be arrested, saying to the chief priests, and captains of the temple, and the elders who were with the mob, "Be ye come out, as against a thief, with swords and staves? When I was daily with you in the temple, ye stretched forth no hands against me: but this is your hour, and the power of darkness" (22:52, 53). And so the company of soldiers seized Him as prisoner and brought Him to trial.

THE TRIALS (22:66 – 23:25)

There were several trials. The first trial was in the
Jewish court where Jesus was brought before the high
priest. Here they wanted to have Him condemned to
death. In Jewish law blasphemy was something for which
a man could be condemned to death, so they accused him
of blasphemy. After failing to get convincing testimony
from witnesses, they questioned Him directly.

> Art thou the Christ? tell us. And he said unto them, If
> I tell you, ye will not believe: And if I also ask you, ye
> will not answer me, nor let me go. Hereafter shall the Son
> of man sit on the right hand of the power of God. Then
> said they all, Art thou then the Son of God? And he said
> unto them, Ye say that I am (22:67-70).

The full force of the Greek words is not felt in the
English translation. His actual answer was very much
like the common idiom today: "You said it." That's
exactly what His words meant, and they understood Him.
"And they said, What need we any further witness? for
we ourselves have heard of his own mouth" (verse 71).

Today when people wonder whether or not Jesus ever
claimed to be Christ, they will turn to this passage. Reading this portion through to the end of the chapter will
show that He said He would be sitting at the right hand
of God. Only the Son of God could sit there! So they
understood him very well. It is no wonder they asked
Him, "Art thou then the Son of God?" When He said,
"Yes, just like you said it," they understood this to be
His claim. There seems no reason that anyone today could
be in any doubt that Jesus of Nazareth plainly claimed to
be the Son of God. This was exactly why they condemned
Him. Right in their presence, He made this very claim.

The practical problem facing the Pharisees and others
who wanted Jesus put to death was that in those days
the Roman government, which was the military government of the country, took away from the local people,

the national people, the Jews in this case, the authority
to put a man to death. This penalty was reserved for
the Roman government. Thus they protected subject na-
tionals against harsh treatment from their own people.
And so, although the Jews had condemned Jesus to death
for blasphemy, they couldn't put Him to death. The
Roman government would have interfered. Instead they
brought Him into Pilate's court and there they accused
Him of treason which was a crime for which death was
the penalty. The Jews did not have any special interest
in Caesar, but they knew that in the Roman court they
could have Him condemned to death for treason, if they
could establish that He was a rival of Caesar. This was
all they wanted. And so, although in their own court
they accused Him of blasphemy and for that reason condemned Him to death, when they brought Him before
Pilate they didn't accuse Him of blasphemy, but of insur-
rection. They accused Him of starting a rival government
in which He called himself a king.

When Pilate began to examine Him, he heard that
Jesus was from Galilee. Herod was king of Galilee, as
Pilate was the governor of Judaea; so Pilate sent Jesus
over to Herod's court. It is quite possible that Pilate did
not want to judge this good man. Pilate apparently was
a man who had some sense of justice, and he knew there
was nothing wrong with Jesus of Nazareth. It seemed he
wanted to avoid having anything to do with what looked
like a frame-up to him, if he could help it. So when he
heard that Jesus came from Galilee he sent Him on over
to Herod who was in Jerusalem at that time.

Herod was glad to see Him, thinking Jesus might
work a miracle for him, or do something extraordinary.
But Jesus of Nazareth did not answer a word. He refused
to put on a show of any kind. He simply remained silent.
Then when Herod found out that the "crime" of which
Jesus was accused had occurred in Jerusalem, not in Galilee, he sent Jesus back to Pilate.

There is one aspect of this event that reveals something more about human nature. "And the same day Pilate and Herod were made friends together: for before they were at enmity between themselves" (Luke 23:12). It seems people often get to be friends in trouble. Herod had been against Jesus of Nazareth. Pilate was being forced to be against Jesus of Nazareth. While it was true Herod and Pilate didn't have any use for each other, yet they were both against the Lord Jesus so much that they became friends from that day on.

Luke goes on to tell the further development of the trial. Pilate called together the chief priests and the rulers and the people, and proceeded with the trial. John points out in his gospel account (19:1-11) that as Jesus stood before Pilate with the chief priests and the elders accusing Him, He answered never a word. They had mocked him. They had beaten Him. They had spit in His face, plucked His beard, beaten Him over the head, had put on a purple robe, mocking Him as king, had plaited a crown of thorns and jammed it on His head. Everything was being done to humiliate Him according to the crude and barbarous fashion of the people of that time. As Jesus stood there before him, Pilate was touched. He was disturbed, because this man had such quietness, such serenity, such peace. Pilate asked Him, "Why don't you answer us? Why don't you defend yourself?" And then he went further. "Don't you know what is happening to you? Don't you know I've got the power to put you to death?" It was then the Lord Jesus spoke up: "Thou couldst have no power at all against me, except it were given thee from above." Pilate knew it was true, and felt all the more uneasiness about condemning this innocent man.

In an attempt to spare Jesus, Pilate went out to these people and said, "I tell you, at this time of the year we always let one prisoner go free. Now I've got in prison here an extremely bad man, Barabbas. He is a man of sedition, a traitor, and a murderer and has caused trouble. He is just a real bad man. Then we have this Jesus of Nazareth." And he knew, as everyone knew, that nothing

could be said against Him; no fault was found in Him.
"I will let one of these go. Which one will you take?"
There need be no doubt that Pilate hoped they would
ask for the good man, Jesus of Nazareth.

When Pilate counted on the sense of justice in people
he made a mistake. People don't do what they know is
right. They do what they want to do. Pilate said, "Which
one will you have?" And they shouted, "Barabbas." Obviously, that was not what Pilate had hoped for. Then
Pilate asked that famous question, "What shall I do then
with Jesus which is called Christ?" (Matthew 27:22). And
the people all said, "Crucify Him." Then they made such
an uproar that Pilate was afraid a mob scene would break
out. He was afraid there would be a riot, and word would
get to Rome that he allowed a man who called himself
a king to escape. Such thinking caused Pilate to feel panic.

In a vain attempt to escape moral responsibility Pilate
washed his hands of the whole matter, a gesture indicating
he was no more responsible. He told the crowd, "His
blood will be on your hands," and they said, "So be it.
His blood will be on our hands." Pilate then had Jesus
scourged as a condemned criminal, beyond all that He
had already suffered. As a final act Pilate sentenced Him
to be crucified.

CARE FOR JESUS' BODY (29:50-56)

As Luke tells the story, after the crucifixion there
comes the brightest light in the whole account. Joseph
of Arimathaea – a businessman, a layman, a man who se-
cretly believed in the Lord Jesus Christ, but who did not
confess Him openly for fear of the Jews, a rich man, a
counselor, and a good man who hadn't consented to their
deeds when they took Him to put Him to death – this man
came to Pilate and said, "Let me have His body." In
that gesture Joseph of Arimathaea stepped out when everyone else had turned away; Jesus' own disciples were at
a distance. All the people had turned against Him, the

soldiers had mocked Him, the rulers had betrayed Him, the soldiers had put Him on the cross. Now comes Joseph of Arimathaea saying, in effect, "That's my Lord. Give Him to me. You don't want Him. You have just killed Him. Give Him to me." He took Him down from the cross and took Him to his own new tomb, where no man had ever been laid, wrapped Him in linen clothing and laid Him away.

It is a sobering thought to realize that the angels in heaven had to stand by while God allowed the soldiers to beat the Lord Jesus Christ. Crude, vulgar people spat in His face and plucked His beard. They blasphemed. They mocked Him. They derided Him and degraded Him in every possible way, and heaven was silent. It was as if God willed: "Let it happen." Jesus bore the whole event in Himself. And finally, as He hung on that cross, they came and pierced His side and there ran out blood and water. There was no direct action from heaven. It is true the earth shuddered in an earthquake: the light of the sun was blotted out for three hours. But no angel came to help Him in that last terrible hour when He died for the sins of the world.

Yet in Luke's account it is obvious from the moment He was crucified, no hands touched Him but the tender hands of those who loved Him. When He was taken down from the cross, this was done by a man who was willing to brave the whole hostile atmosphere, a rich man, a prominent man who came out in the open to do it. And Nicodemus, the man who came to Jesus by night, came and helped Joseph. They wrapped Him in linen cloth, anointed Him with spices, and carried Him away gently, tenderly, lovingly. The Son of God had paid the price, and from then on God moved in to have only His own take care of Him.

All heaven won't be long enough, eternity won't be long enough to hear the praise that will be going up for-ever and ever and ever: "Worthy is the Lamb that was slain . . . and sitteth upon the throne . . . forever and ever" (Revelation 5:12, 13).

Unto Him who loved us and gave Himself for us and washed us in His own blood and loosed us from our sins, and hath made us to be kings and priests unto God, to Him be all the praise, forever and ever and ever and ever.

Throughout all eternity the praise of the Lord Jesus Christ will roll on and on and on and on, because He endured so much for you . . . and for me!

Chapter 10

THE RESURRECTION

The gospel of Luke is a written account by Luke, the beloved physician, of "those things" about Jesus of Nazareth "which are most surely believed among us" to his friend, Theophilus, "that thou mightest know the certainty of those things, wherein thou hast been instructed." The report began with the virgin birth of the Son of God in the form of Jesus of Nazareth and followed in a general way the course of His public ministry. The closing chapter deals with the Resurrection of Jesus Christ. Not only is this the natural place for this event to be set forth, but in a deeper sense this is the crucial point in the whole gospel story. Everything Jesus Christ came to do, every promise in the Word of God holding forth the grace of God, depends on the reality of the Resurrection. Paul wrote that faith in the Resurrection of Jesus Christ from the dead was essential in salvation (Romans 10:9), and in another place said that this was the basis for our confidence in the validity of the Gospel (I Corinthians 15:12-19).

During His earthly ministry Jesus of Nazareth demonstrated the power of God over natural situations and natural conditions. God was shown to be able to control the processes of nature at His will by His Word. The greatest demonstration of such power was in the resurrection of the body of Jesus of Nazareth, and in its eventual ascension into heaven.

The actual event of the Resurrection is reported by Luke in such simple direct fashion that much can be learned from looking at the last chapter of his gospel. Much of what happened in those days shows the truth of the Gospel and of the life in Christ.

THE GREAT CLIMAX (24:1-12)

As Luke tells the story of the various events in his gospel the Resurrection is the great climax: this is the great demonstration of the actual process which produces the difference between "the old man" and "the new man," the resurrection from the dead. The entire old life of any person is to be considered as what is called *dead;* the new life in Christ is truly what is called *life.* Any man who receives this new life through faith in Christ is transferred from death unto life and will now be different in the Lord Jesus. The Resurrection of Christ had to take place to demonstrate actual evidence that God means what He says, as John 3:16 sets forth: " . . . that whosoever believeth in him should not perish, but have everlasting life." In what sense? In the sense that although the old man dies, the new man will live forever.

Luke's report of the Resurrection itself is very simple:

> Now upon the first day of the week, very early in the morning, they came unto the sepulchre, bringing the spices which they had prepared, and certain others with them. And they found the stone rolled away from the sepulchre. And they entered in and found not the body of the Lord Jesus (Luke 24:1-3).

It would be helpful to consider a word of explanation here about the nature of burial in those days. When Jesus of Nazareth was buried it was not like the burial one would see today. Generally speaking, in today's burial the person is put a number of feet under the ground. Usually a casket of steel or other metal or wood contains the body, and the grave is filled in with earth. But that is not the way in which Jesus was buried. In accordance with the custom of the time, the grave was in a cave. Any man who held a respectable position in the community, with sufficient money to do as he wanted, would purchase a cave, and prepare a place for himself and for his family where their bodies might be buried properly.

After death, the body was wrapped in cloth enclosing spices, similar in this respect to the way the Egyptian mummies were treated. After this careful treatment the wrapped body would be laid in a cave. Sometimes this cave would be hewn out of solid rock.

Joseph of Arimathaea had prepared himself such a tomb, a cave in the hillside, and it was ready against the day of his death, as was the custom. These caves were large enough, of course, to contain several bodies. A man could walk into the cave, stooping down to get through the low opening. After a burial the low doorway would be blocked with a slab of stone. Thus, unauthorized people or wild animals would be kept out of the family tomb. Such was the normal custom of burial.

When Joseph of Arimathaea took the body of the Lord Jesus down from the cross, he wrapped it in fine linen and anointed it with spices. This was done by using an ointment mingled with aromatic spices. Then Joseph took that sacred body and laid it in his own new tomb "wherein never man before was laid" (Luke 23:53). It was not uncommon that there would be tombs where the skeletons of a family would be in view as one entered: but this was Joseph's own tomb which had not yet been used. After the body was laid to rest the stone was rolled to the door. Thus the sepulcher was sealed. When the Jews recalled that Jesus had said He would rise on the third day, they went to the governor, and he instructed the guard to close and seal the tomb and put a watch of soldiers there to see that no one disturbed the body.

On the first day of the week, very early in the morning, some of the followers of Jesus came to the sepulcher. The women brought spices because they wished further to anoint His body. Jesus had died late in the day, so there was no time on that evening before the Passover to do this properly. They would have had to complete the task by sundown, the official beginning of Passover. Because this was impossible in the time left on the day

He died, they came early in the morning to complete the work of preparing the body for what they considered its final rest.

Frequently the question is asked about the *three* days. It seems the time need not be exactly seventy-two hours. By common usage the term *three days* has been used to denote the time Jesus was in the grave. Whether this is meant to be precise or not there is no way of knowing, since the days of the week did not bear the names used today. General belief is that Jesus was crucified on a Friday, the day before the Passover, and put into the tomb on Friday afternoon. He was in the tomb all day Saturday, which was the Jewish Sabbath, and then He rose from the dead early on what we would call Sunday morning, the first day of the week. This does not total seventy-two hours, but it involves three separate days and is probably the way things happened.

When the women reached the sepulcher, they found the stone rolled away from the door. When they entered the tomb, the body of Jesus Christ was missing. This would give an indication of the size of the tomb, since they could enter so easily: and the record tells of "Peter . . . stooping down, he beheld the linen clothes laid by themselves . . . " (Luke 24:12). Thus it would seem the height of the tomb was perhaps five or six feet.

When these disciples "found not the body of the Lord Jesus," they were perplexed and disturbed, perhaps even shocked and confused.

And it came to pass, as they were much perplexed thereabout, behold, two men stood by them in shining garments: And as they were afraid, and bowed down their faces to the earth, they said unto them, Why seek ye the living among the dead? He is not here, but is risen: remember how he spake unto you when he was yet in Galilee, Saying, The Son of man must be delivered into the hands of sinful men, and be crucified, and the third day rise again. And they remembered his words, And returned from the sepulchre, and told all these things unto the eleven, and to all the rest. It was Mary Magdalene, and Joanna, and Mary the mother of James, and other women that were with them, which told these things unto the apostles. And their words seemed to them as idle tales, and they believed them not. Then arose Peter, and ran unto the sepulchre; and stooping down, he beheld the linen clothes laid by themselves, and departed, wondering in himself at that which was come to pass (24:4-12).

Peter's attention was drawn especially to the clothing, the very linen cloth in which the body of Jesus had been wrapped, left as it was in the tomb. For any practical person, there would come the realization, as it certainly would to Peter, that no one had stolen the body away, for thieves would not have removed the linen cloth. They would simply have carried the body, as it was, to another place. John's gospel calls attention to the fact that the " . . . napkin, that was about his head, not lying with the linen clothes, but wrapped together in a place by itself" (John 20:7). It seemed obvious someone had handled it, and this was just what must have astonished Peter and the others. The natural explanation would be that Jesus had gotten up and taken the cloth off His head and folding it, put it to one side. The cloth was there to be seen!

Luke reports that Peter "departed, wondering in himself at that which was come to pass." If anyone should be disposed to think that these were prejudiced people, easily impressed, it should be noted that up till now probably no one believed the body was alive. Even Peter went away wondering in himself. He wasn't able to accept what he had been and noted, even as it appeared.

Some of the other gospel accounts tell other items of much interest. They tell about the meeting of Jesus with Mary Magdalene, and how she thought He was the gardener. But just now attention will be directed to a rather lengthy account concerning an incident that only Luke reports.

How He Is Known (24:13-32)

And, behold, two of them went that same day to a village called Emmaus, which was from Jerusalem about threescore furlongs [about eight miles]. And they talked together of all these things which had happened. And it came to pass, that, while they communed together and reasoned, [walking along] Jesus himself drew near, and went with them. [It was not an uncommon thing for a third person, a traveler, to fall in with others along the way, walking with them and making conversation.] But their eyes were holden that they should not know him. [We are not given any explanation as to how that was, whether it was some effect upon them which didn't permit them to interpret what they saw, or whether it was something about the Lord Jesus Himself that looked different from when they had last seen Him. In any case they didn't recognize Him.] And he said unto them, What manner of communications are these that ye have one to another, as ye walk, and are sad? And one of them, whose name was Cleopas, answering said unto him, Art thou only a stranger in Jerusalem, and hast not known the things which are come to pass there in these days? And he said unto them, What things? And they said unto him, Concerning Jesus of Nazareth, which was a prophet mighty in deed and word before God and all the people: And how the chief priests and our rulers delivered him to be condemned to death, and have crucified him. But we trusted that it had been he which should have redeemed Israel: and beside all this, to day is the third day since these things were done. Yea, and certain women also of our company made us astonished, which were early at the sepulchre; And when they found not his body, they came, saying, that they had also seen a vision of angels which said that he was alive. And certain of them which were with us went to the sepulchre, and found it even so as the women had said: but him they saw not. Then he said unto them, O fools, and slow of heart to believe all that the prophets have spoken (24:13-25).

Actually the word *fool* in the Bible relates to a person who does not trust God. It means living in this world as if God did not exist and this whole universe came out of nothing. That is considered to be about as ridiculous as a person can be. This is the real significance of this word *fool*. Jesus called them "fools" here because they didn't believe God's word.

> O fools, and slow of heart to believe all that the prophets
> have spoken: Ought not Christ to have suffered these things,
> and to enter into his glory? And beginning at Moses and
> all the prophets, he expounded unto them in all the scrip-
> tures the things concerning himself (24:25-27).

Passage after passage He brought to their minds and
showed them there was this word through all the Scriptures of God's servant suffering:

> . . . a man of sorrows, and acquainted with grief: and we
> hid as it were our faces from him; . . But he was wounded
> for our transgressions, he was bruised for our iniquities:
> the chastisement of our peace was upon him; and with his
> stripes we are healed (Isaiah 53:3-5).

Jesus showed them that this revelation had been given
over and over and over again: God will send His righteous servant; He will send His chosen one, the Messiah,
the Christ; this one will come to save His people; the
way He will save his people is by suffering for them;
He will die for them; and "by his stripes we are healed."
Throughout Scripture this was the message: God would
forgive sins because of the shedding of the blood of an
innocent substitute. He then showed them that the death
of Jesus had been exactly according to plan.

The one who was crucified is the righteous servant.
Here is the righteous branch of whom Isaiah spoke. Here
is the Messiah, the Prince. Here is the one who does the
will of God, and who is going to save His people. The
way He saves His people is by suffering for them, dying
for them, bearing their sins in His own body. The scape-
goat bore the sins "out of the camp." And in the same
way the Redeemer suffered outside the camp, outside the
city, rejected . . . taking the place of the sinner.

Thus Jesus talked to those two disciples. And as they
approached the village of Emmaus, Jesus "made as though
he would have gone further." Here were two people walking along the road to their home. They were greatly disturbed and distressed. Jesus knew all about this, and He

to walk with them. As He walked with them, He
talked with them, opening their minds to show them that
the calamity that so grieved them belonged in the over-all
plan of God. As these disciples listened, their hearts
burned within them. It is always a heart-warming experience to walk and talk with the Lord. As they came to
the place where they lived, Jesus made as though He
would have gone further. This puts the matter of con-
tinuing in this following directly before them.

Right here is to be seen one of the most significant
insights into the development of spiritual experience. A
person reads the Bible. He hears Bible teaching and
preaching. He hears sermons. He thinks of these things
and the idea grows on him that Almighty God, the Creator
of the heavens and the earth, is interested in each individual. He will save sinners. Wonderful! He sent His Son
to die for sinners. Glorious! The Lord Jesus came and
laid down His life for those who are lost. Marvelous!
And his heart is warmed just hearing these things. And
then, in his thinking he gets to the place where he lives,
where he is involved, and now he has to decide whether
he is going to let Christ Jesus move away. All he has
heard in the Gospel is true, but now the general application is over and he is right down to where he lives.

In this instance with these two disciples, Jesus made
as though He would have gone further. He didn't say,
"Let me stay with you tonight and I'll show you something." He didn't hint around, "It's getting kind of late.
I think I'd like to have a place to stay for tonight."
Abruptly they were confronted with the danger of having
the blessing come to an end. They had had a wonderful
time. It probably had taken them several hours to walk
that distance. They had been talking, listening, talking,
and now it was time to turn in to their home.

This same situation develops when it's time to go
away from the church and go home . . . get dinner ready,
get the children ready for school in the morning, take
care of the laundry, work in the yard, go to work, to the

office and perhaps meet some horrible people and deal with them throughout the day. The blessing found at the church is in danger of fading out until next Sunday. It is at that moment an interested person must speak up and ask for the blessing to continue.

As they had been walking home, Jesus had come to be associated with them. He brought them blessing they had not expected, and now He made as though He would go further. Suppose they had let Him go on? How often have people let Him go away! What a blessedness to have on Thursday morning in the kitchen what was experienced Sunday night at church! This is the real issue. After a person has once had a taste and the Lord has blessed, there seems to come a time when a choice must be made. It will be necessary to ask for continuation.

These two disciples constrained Him. "Abide with us," they said. That was the invitation. They pointed out that it was "toward evening and the day was far spent." They really wanted Him to stay.

"Abide with us." How much is implied in those simple words! One thing seems clear – the disciples did not hesitate to urge Him to stay. Apparently He was not proud nor aloof.

Here is to be seen one of the greatest truths in all the world. The Lord Himself will come to any home. This is certain. He'll come to be with anyone. He'll live with anyone. There is no greater thing! They urged, "Spend the night with us." And He did, just like that! Wonderful, wonderful, wonderful blessing! No questions asked! No one need be afraid of his house being dark. The Lord brings His own light. No one need be afraid about being unworthy. His presence will make it worthy. He'll make it a palace. No one need be afraid about himself. He came for all men. It's the glory of God to share His Presence with the least of His creatures.

The story of Zacchaeus (Luke 19:1-10), to which I referred in Chapter 8, shows this same truth. Because he was a short man, Zacchaeus had climbed up a tree to see who Jesus was as He was coming along in a crowd. Then Zacchaeus had the surprise of his life. He had no idea Jesus of Nazareth knew he even existed, and suddenly Jesus stopped, looked up at him, and was saying He was going to visit in the house of Zacchaeus. It was little wonder that he cried: "No, no, no, Lord, I'm not worthy. My house isn't any good." But Jesus said, "Come on, let's go. I'm going to eat with you." And He did. How long He was in the house with Zacchaeus, the Bible doesn't tell us, but when He left, Zacchaeus, following Him out, said, "Lord, if I have ever taken anything from anyone that I shouldn't have, I'm going to restore it to him fourfold. And from now on fifty per cent of my income I'm going to give to the poor." He did not say this to get rid of Jesus. He said this after he had been with Jesus, doubtless learning of the grace of God. Zacchaeus meant to hold on to the blessing he had found in communion with the Son of God. He wanted Jesus to continue this communion with him all the time. This probably demonstrates the real meaning of what will happen when a person asks the Son of God to continue in fellowship.

Whenever a preacher or teacher has opened the Scriptures to a believer and warmed his heart, the only thing the believer needs to do when he gets home, when it looks as though the echoes of the speaker's voice is fading out of his ears and the atmosphere of the church sanctuary is getting dim, when the Christian gets back into the kitchen or back into the office or into the shop, is to humble and sincerely ask the living Lord, "Lord, don't go. Just stay with me." The marvelous truth is that He'll stay. He did with these people. He went in to tarry with them.

> And it came to pass, as he sat at meat with them, he took bread, and blessed it, and brake, and gave to them. And their eyes were opened, and they knew him; and he vanished out of their sight (Luke 24:30,31).

If anything could emphasize the importance of re-
turning thanks at the table, it would be to remember
that this was the way in which Jesus chose to manifest
Himself to these two people. There was no long, difficult,
elaborate ritual. They did not need to dress up in special
Sunday-go-to-meeting clothes. They were not involved in
an elaborate church service. They were sitting actually
at the table in their own house. Jesus took bread and
thanked God. He returned thanks at the table. "And
their eyes were opened."

This incident shows that the great things of the Gospel
can be opened to a believer in his own home, in his own
room. A person will get to know the Lord there as he will
never know Him anywhere else. This does not discredit
public church services. But the truth is that the Son of
God will show Himself to a believer in his home in a
way much closer than He can ever do in church. He'll
show Himself to a Christian in the privacy of his own
room, in his own life, in his own daily affairs. The Lord
will show Himself to the believer in a very real way.
He is the Saviour. He'll never leave nor forsake anyone
who comes to Him. He died for sinners. He'll keep the
believer forever. This is the glorious truth of the Gospel.

> And they said one to another, Did not our heart burn
> within us, while he talked with us by the way, and while
> he opened to us the scriptures (24:32).

JOYFUL WITNESSES (24:33–53)

When a Christian is stirred in his heart, at church,
in Bible study, in personal testimony, he can rejoice to
know this is of the Lord. That will be the Lord working in him. He can afford to follow such glow. This is
the light he will want to follow until his whole soul is
flooded with the joy of the Lord in fellowship with Him.
All this can be seen in the report of what happened next.

And they rose up the same hour, and returned to Jerusalem, and found the eleven gathered together, and them that were with them, Saying, The Lord is risen indeed, and hath appeared to Simon. And they told what things were done in the way, and how he was known of them in breaking of bread. And as they thus spake, Jesus himself stood in the midst of them, and saith unto them, Peace be unto you. But they were terrified and affrighted, and supposed that they had seen a spirit. And he said unto them, Why are ye troubled? and why do thoughts arise in your hearts? Behold my hands and my feet that it is I myself: handle me, and see; for a spirit hath not flesh and bones as ye see me have. And when he had thus spoken, he shewed them his hands and his feet. And while they yet believed not for joy, and wondered, he said unto them, Have ye here any meat? And they gave him a piece of a broiled fish, and of an honeycomb. And he took it, and did eat before them (24:33-43).

It fell to the lot of Luke, the doctor, to note this bit of scientific evidence that can help to convince anyone that as far as this story is concerned, it means to say that the body of Jesus Christ was actually, literally raised from the dead. A spirit can't eat a piece of honeycomb and a piece of fish. It takes a person with a body to do that, but that's exactly what Jesus did, and for that very reason.

And he said unto them, These are the words which I spake unto you, while I was yet with you, that all things must be fulfilled, which were written in the law of Moses, and in the prophets, and in the psalms, concerning me. Then opened he their understanding, that they might understand the scriptures. And said unto them, Thus it is written, and thus it behoved Christ to suffer, and to rise from the dead the third day: And that repentance and remission of sins should be preached in his name among all nations, beginning at Jerusalem. And ye are witnesses of these things. And, behold, I send the promise of my Father upon you: but tarry ye in the city of Jerusalem, until ye be endued with power from on high (24:44-49).

All of this happened as though He had said, "This is really what I have been trying to tell you. God can raise the dead. And he will raise the dead out of this world into the world to come. For those who put their

trust in Him through Me, this is what will happen. As
God raised Me, so He will raise you. He will raise anyone who believes in Me. Now go and tell it to people
everywhere. They've got sin on their hearts. Tell them
that if they will confess their sins, if they will admit their
need and will believe in God, everlasting life is theirs.
But don't go until you receive the Holy Spirit."

> And he led them out as far as to Bethany, and he lifted
> up his hands, and blessed them. And it came to pass,
> while he blessed them, he was parted from them, and car-
> ried up into heaven. And they worshipped him, and re-
> turned to Jerusalem with great joy: And were continually
> in the temple, praising and blessing God (24:50-53).

Luke ends his account by saying, "Amen" . . . so
be it.

The gospel of Luke presents one of the four accounts
of certain incidents which occurred in the life and death
of Jesus of Nazareth. Some of the events reported by
Luke were also reported by others, some are reported
only by him. Each of the four gospels is written as if it
were the one report being made. This is the character of
eyewitness accounts. Luke did not claim that he personally had been an eyewitness, but he did say that what he
wrote had been delivered unto him by them, "which from
the beginning were eyewitnesses, and ministers of the
word" (1:2). The whole account is written as a simple
record of facts which seemed pertinent to the author. There
are practically no adjectives and no adverbs nor is there
any argument to influence the response of the readers.
The Son of God became incarnate to show forth the truth
of the Gospel of Salvation, and Luke presents Him in
significant action so that each reader in reading these
accounts might "know the certainty of those things,
wherein thou hast been instructed" (1:4).